KING MAKER

APPLYING

DR. MARTIN LUTHER KING JR.'S

LEADERSHIP LESSONS IN WORKING WITH ATHLETES AND ENTERTAINERS

MARCUS "GOODIE" GOODLOE, Ph.D.

#KingMaker

KING MAKER PRAISES

"My knowledge of the author, Dr. Marcus "Goodie" Goodloe, began during his days of leadership demonstrated in the University of New Mexico. From that point forward, I have witnessed the development of his leadership in many arenas including his development in Golden Gate Baptist Seminary where I had the privilege of walking with him in his development as a spiritual leader. When I was asked to read this book, I was pleased to respond to that request. After reading the first draft of King Maker, I found it almost impossible to put it down. My impression was that I had watched "Goodie" write about qualities he found in the national hero "Dr. Martin Luther King Jr." What he discovered in Dr. King, Dr. Goodloe had already demonstrated in his leadership for many years. As I read the manuscript, I was reminded that I had seen these qualities demonstrated already in Goodie's ministry. I am thrilled to recommend this book and will personally recommend to my many friends that they read this wonderful testimony of the things that make leadership kings."

Dr. Bill Crews
President Emeritus
Golden Gate Baptist Theological Seminary

"Nearly fifty years after his untimely death, Dr. Martin Luther King Jr.'s life and legacy continue to challenge us to live up to the ideals this nation was founded upon: justice, equality, and freedom. With God as his guide and a commitment to nonviolence, King recruited people from all walks of life to help champion the Civil Rights Movement, including athletes and entertainers. King Maker brings to the forefront the leadership secrets of Dr. King that are needed for today. A must read!"

Dr. Tony Evans,
Senior Pastor, Oak Cliff Bible Fellowship
President, The Urban Alternative

"Goodie is a friend I value, a leader I respect, and a father I admire. Now I have his concise new book on leadership principles from another hero of mine to promote. What better way to learn King-making than from Dr. Martin Luther King himself? Thanks Goodie for leading us in the way."

Dr. E. Andrew McQuitty, Senior Pastor, Irving Bible Church
Author of *Notes from the Valley: A Spiritual Cancer Travelogue* (Moody Publishers)

"Leadership lessons are best taught through specific examples. In this practical book, Goodie Goodloe digs deeply into the life of a remarkable leader, Dr. King, and pulls out principles the rest of us can learn from. Woven with personal stories from his own journey as a leader, Goodie has crafted an engaging and helpful tool."

Nancy Beach
Leadership Coach, The SlingShot Group
Author of _An Hour on Sunday_ and _Gifted to Lead_

"Drawing from the deep wells of Dr. Martin Luther King Jr.'s wisdom, King Maker offers leaders of faith communities and justice movements, alike, practical guidance on how to organize people, resources, and money toward a better world."

Lisa Sharon Harper
Co-author of _Forgive Us: Confessions of a Compromised Faith_
Chief Church Engagement

"We are so proud to have Dr. Goodie Goodloe as a DBU Ph.D. graduate. His excellent book is a fascinating account of how Dr. Martin Luther King Jr. influenced notable celebrities of his day to join the cause of Civil Rights for African Americans. Not only does Dr. Goodloe's book demonstrate the remarkable wisdom and humility in Dr. King's life and leadership, but it also provides timeless principles for leaders to practice today."

Dr. Gary Cook
Chancellor
Dallas Baptist University

"Dr. Goodie Goodloe, a dynamic preacher and inspiring lecturer, has written an important book on Dr. King's leadership. His study on King's pastoral friendship with famous athletes and entertainers during the time of the Civil Rights Movement expands the horizons of our understanding of King. This is a much-needed book for religious communities as our society looks for new "king-makers" with deep spirituality, creative leadership skill, and prophetic passion for comprehensive social change."

Hak Joon Lee
Professor of Theology and Ethics
Fuller Theological Seminary

Cover Design by Nick Macedo, FirmZero.com
Book Layout & Interior Design by Nick Macedo, FirmZero.com
Cover photo of Goodie Goodloe courtesy of Deep Williams Productions

Scripture quotations are from the Holy Bible, New International Version®, NIV® Copyright © 1973, 1978, 1984, 2011 by Biblica, Inc.® Used by permission. All rights reserved worldwide.
Book Cover
Printed in the United States of America
2015 First Edition
10 9 8 7 6 5 4 3 2 1

Subject Index:
Goodloe, Marcus
Title: King Maker: Applying Dr. Martin Luther King Jr.'s Leadership Lessons in Working with Athletes and Entertainers
1. Leadership   2. Civil Rights Movement   3. Inspirational
4. Christian   5. African-American History

Paperback ISBN: 978-0-996446-7-0-9
Ebook ISBN: 978-0-9964467-1-6

Dream Life Loud LLC
Redondo Beach, CA 90277

kingmakermovement.com

TABLE OF CONTENTS

*To Lucy,
my wife, hero, and best friend
from now to eternity.*

*To Hannah Marie and Joshua C.H.,
you both are cherished gifts from God.
Thanks for letting me be your dad!*

FOREWORD

As one who taught the life and ministry of Dr. Martin Luther King Jr. to seminary students preparing for ministry, I was intrigued with the fresh word and new insights that Goodie Goodloe shares about Dr. King. Goodie writes about the Dr. King we thought we knew. Using very clear language, he introduces us to an easy reading of a book with well researched and well documented stories that makes Dr. King better known and deeper appreciated. The segregated Christians, their pastors, and the poor who marched and went to jail with Dr. King did not underwrite the high cost of freedom.

Goodie explains the leadership skills of Dr. King as a fundraiser and strategist who had cultivated friendships with actors, entertainers, and athletes whose fundraising efforts kept the Civil Rights Movement alive. Teachers of leadership can inform and inspire their students by reading how Dr. Goodloe interprets the leadership genius of the peaceful warrior, author, preacher-orator, scholar and servant leader in Dr. Martin Luther King Jr. You will not regret purchasing this book or more copies to give friends.

The Reverend Doctor J. Alfred Smith Sr.,
Pastor Emeritus,
Allen Temple Baptist Church, Oakland, CA
Professor Emeritus,
American Baptist Seminary of the West, Berkeley, CA

ACKNOWLEDGMENTS

I have been blessed to have advocates, or what I call a supporting cast of family and friends who have served as sources of inspiration and encouragement to me over a lifetime: my mother and godmother, Mary Wagoner and Eugenia Franklin; grandmother, Leotha Coleman; I am eternally grateful to my surrogate parents and mentors Chester F. and Diana Stewart; my mother-in-law, Mara Rosenthal; Bobby Alexander, and mentors Reggie and Delores Lyles, J. Alfred Smith, Sr., Cheryl Elliott, Gary Cook, along with James and Francee Williams. I am indebted to Cole Donohoo, Toby and Shemeka Banger-Hill, Jim Lee, June D'Amour, Ka Mitchell, Kim Rouse, Jason Jaggard (this project moved forward because of you). A special thanks to great sources of wisdom and passion, including Eric and Courtney Kuykendall, Matt and Karen Murrah, Carl and Lisa Winston, my amazing Long Beach California church family: Pastors Joshua and Noemi Chavez of 7th Street Church, and Pastor Mike and Alice Goldsworthy of Park Crest Christian Church. Ryan and Tawny Williams, James and Heather Byun, Fred Harris, F. Chris Garcia, Harvey Collier, Fawn and Zac Woodfin, Danny Noah, Stephen Brown, Kevin Cook, Todd and Alice Salzwedel, Ed Johnson, Dave Bruskas, Sarah Goodson, Dave and Tammy Auda, Jason and Katie Metoyer, Pastors Israel and Rachel Campbell of Wave Church, LA, Mike Williams, Stephen Stoockey, John Jaeger, Adam Wright, Monee Tyler, John Best, and the incomparable musically gifted artists, Soul Fruit. Lastly, but certainly not least, I want to acknowledge the leadership and legacy of Dr.

Martin Luther King Jr., as well as so many other athletes and entertainers who helped pioneer one of the greatest advancements of social change in human history: The Civil Rights Movement.

INTRODUCTION

> I'm still deeply moved inside when I remember myself as a 14-year-old boy listening to Dr. King's "Why I Oppose the War in Vietnam," "The Drum Major Instinct," "Knock at Midnight," and of course, "I Have a Dream."
>
> – Marcus "Goodie" Goodloe, Ph.D.

In my early teens, I remember watching Reverend Jesse L. Jackson, Sr. at a political convention say, "Even though you were born in the slums, the slums were not born in you. You can rise above it, if your mind's made up!"[1] Those words became my internal mantra, my walking theme song, so to speak. I was ready to make something of myself. At that time, of course I had no idea what, but I was determined to bring my best to whatever challenge and opportunity came my way.

Growing up, I loved hip-hop music. I listened to Run DMC, L.L. Cool J, Grandmaster Flash and the Furious Five, The Fat Boys, Kurtis Blow, and Doug E. Fresh. I could spit the lyrics to all of their songs at any moment. I looked forward to borrowing someone's copy of EBONY or JET magazines to read stories and see pictures of popular athletes, black leaders, and celebrities.

As I was coming into adolescence, I read an article in JET about the life and legacy of Dr. Martin Luther King Jr. I was taken aback by the vast impact he had on society in his brief time on Earth – only 39 years. I was fascinated and wanted to learn more. I completed the JET order form and checked off the speeches I wanted. At that time, Dr. King's speeches and sermons were on free cassette tapes, but you had to pay for the shipping and handling. I literally scrounged up pennies from doing chores and begged my mom for the balance to purchase my first series of tapes. Since I didn't have a bank account at that time, I walked down a few blocks to the local grocery store that had a Western Union to buy a money order.

After I received my first set of tapes, I was totally hooked. I ordered tapes regularly. Each time I opened the package and saw the white cassettes with King's speech title in red letters from the Southern Christian Leadership Conference (SCLC), it was as exciting for me as opening presents on Christmas morning. Every night I put a tape into my cassette player and fell asleep, committing to memory some of Dr. King's most significant speeches. I can still hear the crackling sound of the tape and the audience in the background applauding and praising his words: "Amen! Preach brother! Right on! Make it plain!" By that time, the recordings were over 25 years old. I still remember as a 14-year-old boy listening to Dr. King's "Why I Oppose the War in Vietnam," "The Drum Major Instinct,"

"Knock at Midnight," and, of course, "I Have a Dream."

Dr. King was brilliant. He could riff on Plato, Aristotle, Einstein's Theory of Relativity or even Pop-Culture, and then segue into Equality, Justice, Nonviolence, and Love. King quoted from The United States Constitution, the Declaration of Independence, and The Bill of Rights as easily as he did from the Old and New Testaments. I remember thinking, *"Wow, these words are not commonly spoken by anyone,"* at least not anyone whom I knew. As I listened attentively over and over again, I could feel that the audience was not just impacted by his words, but by the values and commitment he embodied. I got the sense people were moving with him in a direction and at a pace they had only imagined, but never acted upon. Dr. King brought to life a realization and opportunity for blacks to follow a new path for their own passion and life narrative.

When I think about my life and what shaped the trajectory of it, until now, most people would not believe that a young boy from Compton waited anxiously for SCLC's envelopes to arrive at my post office. There is no doubt that those countless hours alone listening to Dr. King's tapes shaped my public moments on stage speaking to thousands, and fueled my relentless desire to pursue justice, love, mercy, and to walk humbly with the Creator. That secret investment in my future solidified my investment in others and created a thirst to serve alongside them.

In this book, I bring to light the behind-the-scenes stories of Dr. Martin Luther King Jr. and his work with some of the most famous people of his time to affect positive change in the world. I have also included my first installment list of today's King Makers. Many of the individuals depicted I have worked with, while others are in the public eye making lasting contributions to others in the U.S. and abroad.

I have extracted leadership lessons from Dr. King's relationships with the movers and shakers in two unlikely places: the sports and entertainment industries. Both of these groups are grossly understudied in relation to the Civil Rights Movement from 1954 to 1968. King was strategic and intentional in inviting athletes and entertainers to lend their hands and voices to social action. Simply put, power is the ability to identify and make changes.

King's efforts had substantial implications for one of the most significant social movements in the latter half of the twentieth century. He used his experience and skills as a civil rights leader, minister, academic scholar, and personal admirer of athletes and entertainers to gain their attention. Once they were on board, their influence and power resulted in financial, political, moral, and social support for the Civil Rights Movement.

The A-listers who joined King's "coalition of conscience" included Nina Simone, Mahalia Jackson, Tony Bennett, Charlton Heston, Josephine Baker, Jesse Owens, James Garner, Marlon Brando, Ossie Davis, Jackie Robinson, Muhammad Ali, Harry Belafonte, Joan Baez, Sidney Poitier, Eartha Kitt, Duke Ellington, Josephine Baker, and Dick Gregory. King did not lead athletes and entertainers haphazardly. He calculated his actions in light of the opposition he faced and the potential that remained untapped in rallying some of the nation's most public figures to walk alongside him.

An aura of King's influence in bringing athletes and entertainers to consider their social responsibilities to the nation nearly fifty years ago can be seen today. Athletes and entertainers lead charities and foundations that advocate the importance of reaching at-risk children by running youth programs in urban communities. From local gyms to summer sports camps, professional sports leagues spend millions of advertising dollars to inform the public of investments in their respective cities.

Entertainers have joined elected officials to use their celebrity for social and economic injustices in America and around the world. Neutrality in the face of injustices is no longer *en vogue* and athletes and entertainers have attached their names and resources to causes such as AIDS awareness, poverty, illiteracy, human rights, homelessness, global warming, as well as humanitarian, and natural disaster relief efforts. This type of social consciousness was influenced by King's leadership, directly and indirectly, over forty years ago. The historical narrative of King's efforts to bring social progress through this unique group of individuals is clear, and King deserves credit for such.

Dr. King's leadership rise was unique in that he was not an elected official nor a royal king. Yet his power and influence to disturb the conscience of a nation and to move people of good-will to risk their livelihood and sacrifice their time and money is a testament to his persona. King was able to stretch this exclusive group to greater performances than hitting balls or performing on stages. Instead, he moved their hearts and consciences to help dramatically alter the course of human progress and the scales of justice toward the least counted and often left out. His work was simply remarkable and represents the purest definition of the phrase King Maker, a person of great influence without any royal or political succession.

As you will see, each leadership lesson is more powerful than the next. We all have the opportunity to become King Makers. I pray these pages of timeless stories and leadership wisdom will awaken the King Maker in you. Grab hold of the power. The world is waiting!

> Our lives begin to end the day we become silent about things that matter.
>
> – Dr. Martin Luther King, Jr.

CHAPTER ONE

THE POWER OF
SANKOFA

"It's time we change our perception of history and not look at it as just something that happened in the past, but as something that was deliberately created for us to learn from."

- Marcus "Goodie" Goodloe, Ph.D.

CHAPTER 1

There is an African saying Sankofa, which translated in English, means "reach back and get it." [2] It is usually illustrated by a bird reaching back with its long neck while moving forward. In other words, you need to know what happened in the past to build a successful future. The past should be our source of wisdom where we learn and grow from our experiences and that of others. People choose to relate to the past in several ways. Some relate with cynicism. Why look back? It only stirs up pain and regret. Even the Bible tells us to look forward in Philippians 4. Others see the past as a burden that carries traditions they deem meaningless. Still others, myself included, see the past as a great opportunity to learn, grow, and become better.

Fortunately, my kids are young enough to really enjoy family traditions. Whether it is going to see their grandparents, having dinner as a family, or traditional holiday gatherings, they're all-in. However, I try to prepare myself for the teenage years which may be an entirely different story. So for now, my wife Lucy and I will enjoy these times when the Goodloe Tribe hangs tight and truly has fun sharing stories and enjoying each others company. Now more than ever, it is important for parents to instill traditional family values in their children. Such a practice gives the younger generation a sense of belonging and a meaningful purpose for coming together. It is also a time to share your faith and bring to the forefront any issues or challenges a family member is dealing with. Try to make all of your nuclear and extended family encounters fun, engaging, and memorable. It is the only way your legacy and family history will survive.

• • •

I love to play golf. I'm on a mission to consistently beat my lifelong friend and college roommate Carl Winston. When I'm on the course, I have to keep reminding myself that I've got to have a short memory when I make a bad shot. Forget it Goodie, just forget about it! If I don't say this over and over in my head, one errant shot could lead to the next errant shot and ruin my entire game. That's why I carry around a small tablet when I'm on the course. It contains notes and descriptions of what I did on the previous day's holes, what club I used, and where the ball landed. I often check my notes from past performances so I won't repeat those bad shots, but hopefully improve upon them.

Not coincidentally, in the Christian Scriptures laws were written on tablets. These ancient tablets were designed for the same reason: to pass on guidance from God to humanity. God's laws are our call to remember His Word, which offers us a better life from now to eternity. Perhaps it is because of the eternal nature of God, but in the Scriptures, He sees the past and the future as synergistically linked. The phrase "Remember you were once slaves in Egypt" [3] is found in the same text as "Your young men will see visions and your old men will have dreams". [4] Remembering our past, to God, is a major resource for our future. In fact, the movement of God amongst humanity is one of learning from the past and marching fearlessly into the future.

HISTORY IS OUR STORY

> We have a tendency to repeat the past rather than learn from it.
>
> – Marcus "Goodie" Goodloe , Ph.D.

Dr. King was keenly aware of the African-American struggle. As a young boy and throughout his developmental years, he faced the constant challenges of what it meant to be somewhat less than a second-class citizen in America. King was born in Atlanta, Georgia, the son and grandson of Baptist ministers. Racial segregation, inhumane violence, and inequality of African-Americans were rampant. As a teenager, he was immersed into the affairs of his father's church and became more aware of the African-American plight in America, as his father and grandfather were leaders of the National Association for the Advancement of Colored People ("NAACP"). [5] It was then that his full awareness of the grave economic inequities for his people came to light. He worked alongside his father's leadership campaigns against racial voting discrimination and inequity in teachers' salaries.

King was a student of history. After graduating from Morehouse College, while attending seminary in Pennsylvania, King read everything he could get his hands on about Mahatma Gandhi. He incorporated Gandhi's nonviolent movement with his Christian faith in order to lay a firm foundation for the ultimate success of the Civil Rights Movement. In nearly all of his public speeches, King quoted from The Declaration of Independence and The U.S. Constitution. In King's most famous speech, "I Have a Dream," he stated, "When the architects of our Great Republic wrote the magnificent words of the Constitution and the Declaration of Independence, they were signing a promissory note to which every American was to fall heir."[6]

King viewed that promissory note as a guarantee that all Americans would be afforded "the unalienable rights of life, liberty, and the pursuit of happiness," as stated in the Declaration of Independence. More importantly, this same guarantee of equality was expressed 100 years earlier in Lincoln's Gettysburg Address. King studied these two great historical documents at length. Throughout his life, he relentlessly spoke the words of America's Founding Fathers to highlight the inconsistencies and unfair treatment of African-Americans.

> A people without knowledge of their past history, origin and culture is like a tree without roots.
>
> – Marcus Garvey

He also studied the country's past failures to address the issue of racism, as well as the global challenges of violence, social clashes, and slavery from ancient Rome to Hitler's Germany and later to Vietnam. Unfortunately, America defaulted on the promissory note of the past and continues to overlook racial equality to this day.

TAKING A STAND

To a certain extent, I agree with the cynics who are at odds with a Sankofa mentality. I don't believe the past should be used to distract us from the future, nor should it haunt us like a nightmare by only revisiting events that are negative and painful. I am also against those who relate to the past with an unhealthy sense of nostalgia. That is, remembering it in a more positive light than it actually was in truth and texture, by creating your own narrative of the past that's appropriate for the moment, versus the reality of the choices you made and the resulting consequences. On the other hand, I realize that people sell themselves short with respect to the past and forget important details that matter to help move us to moments of health and wellness.

Sometimes when I open my mouth to talk about Dr. King and The Civil Rights Movement, people give me this incredulous look like, Why on earth do you want to go back there? But that doesn't stop me. I keep talking until they see the need to look at the historic events of the 1960s and what is happeing today through similar lenses. Whether it be racial tensions, poverty, or human rights violations on a national and global scale, the past is clearly relevant.

I challenge you to take the details of the past seriously, so that you can arrive at moments of greatness not by accident- like a "one-hit-wonder." I encourage you not to look at the past as an emotional roadblock that precludes you from taking the necessary steps to move forward in life. Fear, anxiety, worry, and previous failures will cause you to detour on your predetermined road to create something more bold and beautiful than you could ever imagine.

An unfulfilled destiny is a casualty of time lost and the promise and potential for our lives and the greater human community to be served. So to those people who encourage you to have a short term memory, I boldly say, "We can learn from our errors and successes from the past to help us move wisely in the present."

Sankofa.

A few years ago I was traveling to Chicago and the co-pilot addressed the cabin to inform passengers of the violent weather awaiting us at O'Hare Airport. I recall having a brief conversation with the Captain as I was standing in the cabin entry.

"How are things looking?"

"Don't worry. I've been where we're going." He replied confidently.

It turns out that this was his repeat leg of the flight so he knew of the pending pockets of turbulence, altitude, speed and the wind shears to make the necessary adjustments. His words and actions reminded me that

so often we forfeit a smoother ride on the journey of life because we don't look to people who have been there before – we don't take advantage of their experience. There's great value in learning from people who have been there before.

Sankofa.

UNSUNG LEADERS OF OUR PAST

When it comes to the Civil Rights Movement, there are a few great leaders who are still with us today like John Lewis, Andrew Young, and Harry Belafonte. John Lewis walked with King on the Edmund Pettus Bridge in 1965 to affirm voting rights for African Americans and played a key role in the Student Nonviolent Coordinating Committee (SNCC). Lewis has served as a member of the U.S. House of Representatives for Georgia since 1986, and in 2010, he received the Presidential Medal of Freedom Award.

Andrew Young served as a top lieutenant to King and the Southern Christian Leadership Conference (SCLC). Young also served as a member of the U.S. House of Representatives for six years. After his service in Congress, he was appointed as United States Ambassador to the United Nations by then President Jimmy Carter. With the support and encouragement of Coretta Scott King and others, Young ran for the mayor of the city of Atlanta and won two terms. Like Lewis, Young became a recipient of the Presidential Medal of Freedom Award.

Harry Belafonte, the multi-talented, world-renowned star, is considered by many scholars to have had a more significant impact than any other entertainer

in the Civil Rights Movement. Belafonte worked closely with King toward the advancement of King's effort to bring justice and equality to millions of disenfranchised African-Americans. Other contemporaries of King who are still alive today include civil rights leader and two-time presidential candidate Reverend Jesse Lewis Jackson Sr., comedian and activist Dick Gregory, and the award-winning musical artist and activist Joan Baez.

These are just some of the people who we can undoubtedly learn from: they thrived in extraordinary circumstances because they were able to navigate the terrain of social upheaval and social injustice that was as common as the rising sun during King's leadership. These seasoned men and women were part of seismic shifts and quantum gains for our nation's redemption. Yet the journey is far from over and their lessons and wisdom are needed more today than ever before. Stop. Think. Really take a close look at our ugly past so we can move forward to a brighter future.

Sankofa.

INSPIRING OTHERS TO BELIEVE

KANIKA WHITE, Ed.D.

PRINCIPAL
CLINTON ELEMENTARY

COMPTON UNIFIED
SCHOOL DISTRICT

http://web.compton.k12.ca.us/
Pages/Administration/SchoolSites.aspx#

Kanika White never let the labels hold her back. She is a product of teen parents who abused alcohol and drugs that negatively impacted their lives as well as that of their children. Kanika was often left to fend for herself and younger brother. As a foster youth in Compton, CA, the odds of success were not in her favor. White credits her first grade teacher with encouraging her to be accountable for her actions, maintain a strong work ethic, persevere, and not make excuses. White excelled along her educational path in the Compton Unified School District, yet upon graduating, she was ill-equipped for college courses. It was at that moment that she charted her course to become an educator. White went back to the district she grew up and served as kindergarten, 1st, 4th grade, and resource teacher for several years. Her desire to be more impactful led her to a district level administrative position which allowed her to directly impact 16 schools. White's desire to return to the district where she was educated to ensure that children are thoroughly prepared to excel makes her a King Maker, living out her Sankofa assignment. Thank you Principal White.

COALITION OF CONSCIENCE

> Too many of us are looking for our moment on the bus, when we should be spending more time behind the scenes strategizing how to eliminate the real "vehicle" blocking our progress toward justice.
>
> – Marcus "Goodie" Goodloe, Ph.D.

The United States is still plagued with issues that demand collective effort—a coalition of conscience. This essential mindset requires people with goodwill who are committed to redeeming the soul of America. Racial and ethnic tensions remain high in urban communities. We should all pay more attention to the hunger and poverty statistics that continue to rise at record numbers. No longer should we sit idly while our nation's wealthy 1% live incomprehensible lifestyles of luxury and waste.

The "evil triplets," racism, materialism, and militarism, which King discussed two generations ago, should be the

new slogan for human survival. The leaders of the Civil Rights Movement made great strides towards redemption. These men and women along with Dr. King initiated a turning of the tide, a revolutionary change and social transformation in our country. It was a tremendous time as incredible progress was made, progress that brought together some of the most influential people in society.

In school, we all learned about Rosa Parks and the iconic moment when a decision not to change seats on a bus shifted the conscience of a nation. But what most people don't know is her courage started long before she got on that bus. Rosa Parks wasn't surprised by the request from the bus driver. Nor were her actions a spontaneous moment of courage to refuse to sit in the back.

Parks engaged in undocumented meetings and conversations with other Montgomery, Alabama citizens, who were angry with the ugly system of racial inequality that ravaged the heart and soul of the community. Few ever knew that Parks was working in conjunction with activists, and on that particular day, she chose to sit in a "white" seat as part of a brilliant, yet risky strategy implemented by the grassroots organization whose desire was to raise awareness of the racial injustice in Montgomery.

I believe that the more fascinating leadership lessons come from history's untold, yet later revealed secrets. What we often fail to realize is that the untold stories which later come to light are equally important and shape the world as profoundly as the memorable ones in our history books. These types of behind-the-scenes moments of leadership provide the most practical and applicable lessons for our everyday lives as leaders,

because more often than not, we get a glimpse of a great leader demonstrating human fallibility. In fact, if it were not for uncovering these private moments, the public ones might never have materialized.

That's the hidden inequality of our understanding of leadership. We only see the public moments: the victories, the parades, and the successes. When young men and women see or hear a leader speak to thousands, they think, I want to do that someday. What they don't realize is that a leader speaking from a massive platform addressing thousands is only 10% of what the leader does. Not many are privy to bear witness to the thousands of other challenges and disappointments a leader endures out of the spotlight. Yet, seeing and hearing the exponential change that came from one memorable speech, which is the result of overcoming several obstacles, viewers see only the surface, which appears to be a good gig.

What we tend to miss out on are the scores of decisions made beforehand that set these events in motion and prepare these leaders to stand in the light for that purpose in that season. Many of us are eager to practice being in the limelight and long to burn like a fire in the night. But when it comes to examining history, we can miss the sparks that created the flame.

It was an intentional strategy and the bravery of a collective action that led up to Rosa Parks' moment in history. As I stated earlier, too many of us are looking for our moment on the bus when we should be spending more time behind the scenes strategizing how to eliminate the real vehicle blocking our progress toward justice. It's time we change our perception of history and not look

KNOW THEM BY THEIR FRUIT...

SOULFRUIT

RECORDING ARTISTS

HOUSTON, TX

SOULFRUIT.NET

For more than 20 years, Toby, Vanessa, Ty, and Andres have provided a breath of fresh air to audiences around the country delivering God's truth and sharing their musical gifts of hope and joy with impeccable harmonies and memorable choreography. Soulfruit embodies the full expression of what happens when people live and love according to the life and purpose offered by our Creator. In their song, *The Art of Distinction*, they remind us of the importance of making every day count:

"I think today I will try
To make the best day of my life
Take advantage of my time
And do everything right
Good morning
There's no room for sleeping late
The sunrise just doesn't wait
Grab a ray to wash my face
History awaits."

Soulfruit are Kingmakers, and now more than ever before, the world needs not only their music, but the movement they have created.

at it as just something that happened in the past, but as something that was deliberately created to help us learn. There is still a lot more work to do. Reach back. I'm sure you'll be able to find the King Maker in you.

What is your Sankofa call to action?

Why is it important to you?

What are you going to do to live out your Sankofa?

I trust that you will ponder these questions in your search for your own revelation as to the importance of the past. Consider how other individuals, leaders, and events can inspire you to advance to new levels. Every step you make toward a better future for equality, quality of life, and survival for those in your community and ultimately those abroad, will require taking a step back to see how things were done in the past. Did change happen? Why did it happen? What worked? What didn't? Why?

Sankofa.

CHAPTER TWO

THE POWER OF
REQUESTS

"If you want to go fast, go alone, but if you want to
go far, go with others."

- **Mosaic LA**

CHAPTER 2

One of the privileges I've had over the last several years has been leading and serving alongside others within various faith communities in a number of cities, including Los Angeles, Dallas, Kansas City, Albuquerque, and Oakland. During that time, I've found one constant: people have an amazing capacity to respond to great requests when asked. Faith communities are heavily dependent upon volunteers. The greatest asset to mankind on the planet is the human resource. In fact, some of the most beautiful expressions of people joining together for movements and causes greater than themselves have happened in communities of faith. Dr. King's efforts started in the church and attracted volunteers on a national and international scale. I've started my King Maker Movement in the church and have been blessed to raise the platform on stages worldwide.

As a pastor, I frequently called upon the assistance of volunteers. Sometimes, we needed volunteers for their sheer grit and human power in order to get something done. It's hard work setting up and tearing down equipment for over five thousand people at least four times a week. At other times, we called upon volunteers to share their high level of vocational skills, creativity, and expertise to move a project forward; there's no substitute for good old-fashioned brain power. As a result, every aspect of our faith community was enhanced, including our music, pre and post production tasks, social media, as well as special events.

When I think about it, I am amazed at those times when I led hundreds of volunteers for a specific cause. These were dedicated people who did not come on board for fanfare or fame. Oftentimes, their service meant they had to arrive early and stay late. Our volunteers served in capacities that were all too often unattractive: cleaning up dirty restrooms from the previous night's usage during a concert or setting up tables and chairs. Other needs included moving in heavy music, lighting, and audio equipment for a live band, or setting up a prop and designer background sets for drama sketches to be performed during the worship experience. In sum, more often than not, volunteers were asked to work behind the scenes to do what was critical to the overall success of what needed to be accomplished.

Most times, I was challenged to identify creative and tangible ways to express my appreciation for the labor and commitment they provided. With a limited budget, I remained at a constant deficit, and a simple "thank you" or firm handshake or high-five was all I could offer. I learned that in most cases, those simple gestures were all they needed.

> ❝ No man is an island entire of itself...
> – John Donne

Those are hardly the words one would expect to hear from a leader, especially a leader of the caliber of Dr. Martin Luther King Jr. A key characteristic for a leader is to remain stoic in spite of the most challenging situations. Leaders are to appear brave for the public even though they are internally wrestling with the difficulties they face. Why would anyone want to follow someone who lacks confidence in the pursuit of success for the cause at hand? Why would you follow someone who folds under stress? Whether you are leading a church, a Fortune 500 company, a small business, or your own household, it can be a pressure-laden road that must be traveled alone, and the success or failure rests squarely on the shoulders of one man or woman.

King was not immune to the difficulties of leadership we still face today. There were external challenges such as a lack of funding and resources to get things done. He struggled internally with whether he was cut-out to lead the nation for such an important and life-altering cause. In one interview King recalled how there were times he wanted to withdraw and remove himself from the center of the Civil Right Movement, but through prayer and encouragement from others, his resolve was strengthened.

King also had to manage internal stakeholders, politics, and relationship building. Other challenges he faced included motivating people to come on board and remain committed to the cause. As the Civil Rights Movement gained strength and momentum, he faced increasing pressure and the weight of responsibility for the entire African-American community on his shoulders. Where would we be if King quit because the burden was too heavy to bear? Thankfully, King knew the cause was not about him. Likewise, it's not about you!

After the success of the Montgomery boycott, King flew to Harlem, New York to meet with U.S. Representative Adam Clayton Powell Jr. and other African-American community leaders. The purpose of the meeting was to discuss the dehumanizing conditions African-Americans faced in the South. King was given a hero's welcome. While in New York, he attended a number of mass rallies including one at Madison Square Garden and another at Gardner Taylor's Concord Baptist Church in Brooklyn. Over 10,000 thousand people lined the streets in an attempt to gain access to Taylor's church to hear King. A fundraiser service was held in honor of the one-year anniversary of the Montgomery victory. Collection plates gathered over $4,000 for the Montgomery Improvement Association.

King's visit to New York was successful and he gained celebrity status. He was awestruck by his Northern followers. As a result, New York's socially elite put plans in motion for a benefit concert later that year. King and the cause that the SCLC were committed to champion became the benefactors of their financial generosity of key influencers. Immediately, money from the North was being sent to the South without King's solicitation. A national movement was born.

During his trip to New York, unbeknownst to many, King requested a private meeting with actor and singer Harry Belafonte at Adam Clayton Powell Jr.'s church. Belafonte had gained national success in the entertainment industry at the time, but he was no stranger to social and political activism. As a college student,

Belafonte picketed outside the courtroom against the treatment of W.E.B. DuBois during a state trial. Belafonte became an active member of the communist-created Progressive Party Movement. He was very vocal against racism in America.

HOW TO ASK

> "I had to see what this young prophet, and new man from Galilee, would bring to the plight and conditions of African-Americans in the North, the South, and the entire nation." [7]
>
> – Harry Belafonte

Despite his political activism, Belafonte was far from a guaranteed supporter of King. Like other activists and celebrities in the northern part of the country, Belafonte knew of King and had even sent money to support the Montgomery Bus Boycott. Yet he retained a skeptical curiosity of King's ability to successfully lead the nonviolent action campaigns in larger, more populated cities.

Belafonte was also concerned about King's name

recognition.[8] Compared to Powell, Du Bois, and Roy Wilkins of the NAACP, King was a little-known preacher from the South. Like other ministers, King's leadership was nurtured in the bosom of the local church, specifically the African-American church tradition. From the start of his local pastorate and throughout the Civil Rights Movement, King was committed to changing the perceptions and expectations of sharing the message and teachings of Jesus, as seen in the gospels. With respect to political and social problems, negative perceptions ranged from irrelevance to aloofness, which could be seen in the friction among African-American communities, based upon socioeconomic status.

King clearly knew that celebrity endorsements would go a long way in promoting the civil rights cause on its burgeoning national stage. A lot was riding on this meeting and King wanted more than an endorsement from Belafonte. King was aware that Belafonte cared deeply about the race struggle.[9] It was King's humility and offstage personality that won Belafonte over. Belafonte saw first-hand King's willingness to do whatever was necessary in order to advance the cause of justice and freedom.

"I need your help," King said. "I need your help," he repeated. "I have no idea where this movement is going." [10]

In that moment King chose to exert his courage through humility and honesty. Doing so demonstrated his compassionate side, which is an all-too-common shortcoming of strong leaders: making others feel desired. King's assertion that he needed Belafonte's help did not communicate a sign of leadership weakness– far from it.

Rather than a lack of strength, asking for Belafonte's help created an invitation for the entertainer's partnership in the cause, one that led to a high level of ownership and participation on Belafonte's part.

There lies a direct correlation between King's willingness to ask for help and the support of others for the movement, particularly among those of high personal wealth and influence. Now with Belafonte in his corner, he and King were able to persuade this group of elite individuals that they were needed to advance the movement.

A few months later a New York based grassroots civil rights organization, "In Friendship," followed through with its pledge to host a benefit rally on May 24, 1956, in Madison Square Garden. The headliners were Coretta Scott-King, Duke Ellington, and Harry Belafonte. The concert would be the first of many to come given by prominent entertainers and athletes. While their charitable response came in light of King's proven success in Montgomery, their sustained commitment to the movement came largely in part to an understanding that their participation was vital to its success. Again, they were convinced that they were needed. This all came about because of King's power of request.

• • •

When I played football in college I hated the weight room. Maybe it was the smell. Maybe it was because we lifted weights at 7:00 AM every morning. Or maybe it was because every time I attempted a new weight or routine I was compared to everyone else. Either way, there were

STRIKEOUT TO SERVE

CLAYTON KERSHAW

FOUNDER

KERSHAW'S CHALLENGE

KERSHAWSCHALLENGE.COM

Clayton Kershaw is a left-handed pitcher for the Los Angeles Dodgers. He is also a three-time Cy Young Award winner and the 2014 National League Most Valuable Player. As the founder of Kershaw's Challenge, a Christ-Centered organization, he and his wife have partnered alongside other organizations to challenge others to make a difference in the world using their gifts and talents. Their sole purpose is to give back to people in need. To date, they have transformed the lives of children in the U.S. and abroad. In Los Angeles, they provide housing to families as well as animal companionship to at-risk youth. In the Dallas area, they provide after-school sports activities. On an international level, they have built housing and a school in Zambia, Africa, for poverty-stricken youth, and will be venturing out to serve youth in the Dominican Republic. Consider yourself challenged: Do something to help make the world a better place and serve with a true King Maker, in Clayton Kershaw.

plenty of other things I would rather have done with my time than lift weights.

Running was also part of the training for players, and coaches made sure we understood it to be a viable option for punishment and discipline, as well. But lifting weights was something altogether different. I recall the countless moments of exhaustion and muscle fatigue after lifting forty-five pound slabs of steel up and down off my chest or, from the ground, and over my head. I had to work hard and develop an appetite for pushing myself to the limit.

If a person was going to come to the University of New Mexico and be part of our football program, it was not because our weight room had a juice bar and surround sound.

Our weight room was simple; there was absolutely no fluff: we had a few bench presses, squat racks, dumbbells, mats, and medicine balls. This was well before the dawn of nationwide college football programs impressing players with elaborate athletic facilities and playing fields. The equipment looked average at best. The floor mats were stained from countless hours of wear and tear, not to mention mounds of sweat and hand-grip chalk. Music blaring for our inspiration came from a borrowed system belonging to one of the equipment managers. It seemed that there were light fixtures and ceiling tiles that needed to be repaired weekly.

The walls were white, and one side contained a white bulletin board that had black lettering near the front door: "No loud music," "No horse play," and "No food or drink allowed." Sounds like a lot of fun, right? On another wall, there was one rule that was written in red: DO NOT ATTEMPT TO LIFT A WEIGHT WITHOUT A SPOTTER. Of course in a fit of testosterone, guys would often try to lift more than they were capable of. Without a spotter they'd be in way over their heads.

Confronting unfair and unequal treatment of African-Americans under the law during the Civil Rights Movement was too enormous of a burden to be lifted by one person or group. King could not do it alone. The SCLC could not do it alone. Spotters were needed.

Advocating for fair and impartial voting rights was too big of a challenge to be taken on by a mere fraction of the total citizens in the South. Instead, the entire nation's moral strength was needed. Spotters were needed. King knew this to be true and acted accordingly. He believed in the community of humanity. A spotter is ones safety net. King wasn't too proud to ask for a spotter.

I GOT THIS...

Sadly, leaders rarely ask for help when they are the ones most likely in need of it. All too often they choose the path to preserve their pride, rather than humble themselves and consider the betterment of others or the organization as a whole. One of the weakest expressions of a person's character is his unwillingness to ask for help. The sustainability of the Civil Rights Movement in the face of such tremendous adversity was directly related to how many people King invited to partner with him. It was too big to do alone, which was perfectly fine with King.

Many leaders find themselves falling victim to the "I got this" syndrome. We see it all the time in basketball. The lone player dribbling the ball down the court meets one or two defensive players, and instead of passing the ball to a teammate, he actually calls for his team to back off, because of a selfish "I got this," spirit. The player then attempts to ward off the defense one-on-one which usually ends up in a turnover. Such overconfidence stems from a belief that success is a more likely outcome without the help of a teammate.

Too often leaders allow the "I got this" syndrome to go untreated, and they strut through life with this inflated view of self that fosters a distorted reality on three fronts:

When you operate from an unwillingness to admit you need help, you are only fooling yourself. You are short-changing your true potential. Admitting you need help brings you greater credibility. The credibility you gain by asking for help puts you in a teachable posture and moves you into alignment with the rhythms of passion and purpose in your life within the context of community, rather than isolation. By creating opportunities for others to partner with you, you set yourself up to not simply go fast, but go far.

I.   They are lulled into thinking they know everything, including falsities like they are invincible, even when the challenges they face are beyond their given expertise and resources. This is certainly not courage in the face of adversity. A good friend once mentioned to me that courage, at its core, is not an absence of fear, but an absence of self. It is a willingness to sacrifice whatever it takes for the sake of others. Dr. King was arguably one of the most courageous human beings of our time.

II. Leaders communicate to everyone else that they are not necessary. A leader may be successful doing things on his or her own for a short while, but runs the risk of conditioning the team for failure in future crises. Lack of role clarity and feeling unwanted causes teams to collectively disengage. Unfortunately, by the time these types of leaders realize they need help, they are in dire straits because the team has abandoned them. Self-absorption caused them to miss out on greater opportunities had they worked alongside others.

III. Leaders wear a mask to cover insecurity. As human beings we are mortals, which means we have frailties. Insecurity ranks high on the list of leaders who exert a powerful, strong exterior. Internally they are struggling with issues from their past and have learned to hide behind the tough exterior so that everyone will believe they are strong, which in their minds equates to being a good leader. These types of leaders are convinced that they must go at it alone because onlookers will deem them as incompetent.

When you operate from an unwillingness to admit you need help, you are only fooling yourself. You are short-changing your true potential. Admitting you need help brings you greater credibility. Simply put, it let others know, you are not just a one-person boss, and your goal is to embrace a collective effort of others. The credibility you gain by asking for help puts you in a teachable posture and moves you into alignment with the rhythms of passion and purpose in your life within the context of community, rather than isolation. By creating opportunities for others to partner with you, you set yourself up not to merely go fast, but go far.

HERE TO SERVE

JOSHUA + NOEMI CHAVEZ

LEAD PASTORS

7TH STREET CHURCH
LONG BEACH, CA

7THSTREETCHURCH.COM

Joshua and Noemi are the dynamic duo within the Los Angeles faith community! They began as church planters in 2007, and now lead one of the most progressive multi-ethinc communities of faith in Long Beach, 7th Street Church. As pastors, they are committed to bringing the message of faith, hope, and love beyond the pulpit into the hearts and minds of people. The 7th Street Church has partnered with the city police, local after school arts and education programs, as well as the city's child protective services. As part of Pastors Josh and Noemi's commitment to serve, each month they launch a "Missionary for a Day" trip to Mexicali. These trips engage the community with construction projects, maintenance, personal care, and impactful ministries to the youth. The "Celebrate Recovery Program" which helps those struggling with life controlling habits and hurts is a lifeline to the community. In addition to their daily pastoral responsibilities, Noemi travels the country as a national speaker, and Joshua is a dynamic recorded worship leader. My family and I have had the privilege of serving alongside them in a number of capacities in recent years. Every time we are with Team Chavez we realize we've been in the company of King Makers!

WHAT'S YOUR ASK?

It takes courage to ask for help and genuinely embrace the involvement of others. King was willing to ask Harry Belafonte for help even as the Montgomery Bus Boycott was deemed a success. He knew he had more uphill battles to fight which would be critical to the advancement of the Civil Rights Movement. The lesson that must be learned from the life of Dr. King is that regardless of our journeys, no matter how far, how difficult, or the duration of struggle involved, we need others. More importantly, we should both communicate and demonstrate that they are needed and highly valued. Asking for help was part of King's DNA.

CHET'S "ASK"

My mentor and father figure, Chet Stewart of Albuquerque, New Mexico, exemplifies the characteristic of a leader who's willing to ask for help. In 1967, he found himself at the critical juncture in life of taking over the family business. His grandfather, French Stewart, of French Mortuary, was thrilled to have Chet join the family business after completing his mortuary certification and training. Chet and his grandfather entered into a formal partnership one year later. A full-page ad was placed in the local paper to announce the enhanced services French Mortuary would offer.

Three days later, however, Grandpa French died unexpectedly of a major heart attack. At the age of twenty-six Chet was left to run the family business alone. Chet received the news of his grandfather's passing while he was shaving. According to Chet, the next few months proved to be some of the most challenging of his life. One of the first things Chet did after his grandfather died was gather the employees to let them know how much he valued them. He spoke with honesty and humility and admitted that their experience and knowledge of the business far outweighed his own. He promised, as their leader, to be fair-minded and work harder than anyone else, but made it very clear he would rely on their experience, expertise, and insight. He let them know at the outset they were needed.

Once he garnered the collective support from the employees, Chet enlisted the help of Charles Eshleman, an accountant who eventually became a close friend and employee for nearly fifteen years. Chet relied on Charles' advice and wise counsel. Chet paid him $650.00 a month, which was one-hundred and fifty dollars more than he paid himself.

Chet knew it was money well spent. He was faced with pending financial debt and needed a loan from the local bank, Albuquerque National, to keep the mortuary afloat. A $500,000 dollar loan, especially to a 26-year-old kid, was a lot of money back then. However, the president of the bank told him that his grandfather had built up the family name so he was good for the loan. Chet prayed daily for wisdom while onlookers and the competition were convinced he would fail. The odds were stacked against him because of his youth and inexperience.

Since the summer of 1967, French's Mortuary has continued to grow. The company ranks in the top ten of independently owned funeral services in the country and it is the largest in the state of New Mexico. It has an annual budget of ten million dollars and has nearly one hundred-fifty employees. French's Mortuary has won numerous awards, including the 2002 Ethics and Business Award given by the National Samaritan Counseling Center and the Del Norte Ethics Award of New Mexico. Chet served as president of the New Mexico Funeral Association and was named National Mortician of the Year in 1976.

In 2007, French Mortuary became one of only a handful of companies in America to have had only two CEOs in a span of one hundred years. It's hard to imagine the growth and successful legacy of French Mortuary being a reality without the leadership of Chet Stewart. The values and work ethic he instilled help foster continued growth of the company even after his retirement. That legacy and growth began, albeit unexpectedly, with a simple ask for help from someone Chet could rely on and learn from, even though he was the leader of French Mortuary.

Asking for help is one of the greatest demonstrations of power; it requires a posture of humility. We are more human than at any other time when we are humble. When we admit we do not have all the answers, we have a true starting point from which to build. When we are humble we are closer to our truest created form than any other posture or attitude we adopt.

· · ·

Creating an opportunity for those of great influence to partner with him allowed King to advance the cause of civil rights exponentially further than he could have done alone. His willingness to ask ultimately served to see his mission and supporter base grow. Take some time out of your day to honestly respond to these questions:

What is your "Ask?"

What is your "Ask" strategy?

What are you struggling with internally?

What are you committed to doing that would benefit from partnering with others?

When will you "Ask"?

It is my hope these questions will help release you from the myth that says to be a strong leader you must lead alone. I am convinced that the genesis for athletes and entertainers who became deeply ingrained in the cause for social justice during the Civil Rights Movement began with King's request to meet with Belafonte in that New York church basement. The greatest good you could ever do for your organization, your community, or your cause, is to share the burden with others who will partner with you.

.

CHAPTER THREE

THE POWER OF
COMMUNICATION

"People fail to get along because they fear each other;
they fear each other because they don't know each
other; they don't know each other because they have
not communicated with each other."
– Dr. Martin Luther King Jr.

CHAPTER 3

Part of what I get to do for a living is speak to large audiences. I am blessed to travel around the country and stand in front of thousands of people and do my best to educate and inspire. Being a great leader and being a great communicator go hand-in-hand. King ranks high on the list of the greatest orators of all time. His "I Have a Dream" speech has been cited by scholars of American History as a powerful game-changer along the likes of Abraham Lincoln's "Gettysburg Address" and Patrick Henry's "Give Me Liberty or Give Me Death." King's ability to capture listeners and motivate them to act was second to none. He used all of the necessary leadership skills to communicate effectively such as i) building audience trust, ii) showing empathy for the audience and the suffering of others, and iii) having a definite message.

BUILDING TRUST

From the time he was a young boy, King worked alongside his father and grandfather at Ebenezer Baptist Church: "train up a child in the way he should go".[11] His father traveled to a Baptist meeting in Berlin and learned of Martin Luther's defiance of the Roman Catholic Church's false doctrines and was deeply impacted by Luther's stance. So much so that King Sr. changed his name from

Michael to Martin Luther. He also changed the name of his eldest son from Michael to Martin Luther King Jr. [12]

Young Martin read scriptures on Sunday mornings and led various programs at church. He grew up with men he admired who were constantly on center stage speaking to large audiences.[13] As he matured, it was a natural progression to want to become a minister. He was very comfortable speaking and mesmerized listeners when he spoke because of his passion and knowledge of the Bible and history. His active participation in leading the church provided him with credibility and trust that made those outside his community feel good about following him.

As a pastor, he spoke with confidence and authority, offering the congregation hope for a better tomorrow according to God's Word. King became masterful at encouraging people as he moved from the pulpit, to lecture halls, to jail cells, and standing before heads of state. He worked hard to develop the art of preaching and consensus building as he led communities in the nation during the Civil Rights Movement.

EMPATHY

King used compelling stories of empathy and courage from the Holocaust era to vividly capture the challenges the Jewish population endured and how their struggles and those of African Americans were relevant to the times. The power of stories and the narrative of those who sacrificed and suffered years earlier infused action into significant conversations with the nation during the civil rights struggle. Horror stories of the nation's historical treatment toward African-Americans and situations he personally witnessed, bolstered his vision for a new America. One in which people would be judged—not by the "color of their skin, but rather by the content of their character," as expressed in his infamous "I Have a Dream" speech. Nearly every word spoken utilized transformational themes of us and our past, present and future. In other words, we're all in this together. King was an ordinary citizen, just like you and me, yet he accomplished extraordinary feats to preserve human rights for all of us.

Athletes and entertainers were part of King's overall plan to transform the character of the nation and to create a new chapter in American democracy. He used his power of persuasion and called upon Muhammad Ali, Harry Belafonte, Joan Baez, Mahalia Jackson, Sammy Davis Jr., Lena Horne, and countless others of influence and affluence. He knew that if people heard their stories of struggle, they would be moved to action. King needed these high profile individuals to lend their voices, skills, talents, and resources to join with other citizens in what he referred to as the "second revolution"—one of peace and values.

Joan Baez spoke of King's impact and his ability to persuade others, including her involvement in the movement. In an interview with award winning author and historian Taylor Branch, Baez stated, "Martin Luther King, Jr., was cool in a way... I remember Martin would say the word "nonviolent," and I would cry right through the end of his speech. I got all tense because I couldn't believe this man was doing this and giving us all an opportunity to do something decent."[14] Like Ms. Baez, countless others were moved to tears when Dr. King spoke. He had a way of stirring up our inner calling to take action.

CLEAR MESSAGE

> History will have to record that the greatest tragedy of this period of social transition was not the strident clamor of the bad people, but the appalling silence of the good people.
>
> – Dr. Martin Luther King, Jr.

From the genesis of the civil rights movement to the sunset of his life, Martin Luther King Jr. spoke with clarity and conviction. One of the central themes of his leadership message was this: the nation was in need of a radical reordering of its priorities. King sought to engage old alliances and forge new ones, all in an effort to redeem the soul of America.[15] His priority was to move the nation forward on matters of justice, peace, and equality. This was a constant challenge from the early days of the Montgomery Bus Boycott to his final year in addressing matters of war and peace.

His appearance on national television on February 8, 1967, and his speech to business leaders the night before, underscored King's willingness to forge ahead in his quest for what he called a beloved community. The social, political, and economic landscapes had shifted, and King was now unpopular. He needed new strategies to engage the nation. King was determined to prove that the movement he led was still relevant and that the moral condition of the nation demanded that all people of goodwill reaffirm their commitment to building a just and more peaceful union. King's message specifically to athletes and entertainers was clear: success and affluence was not an opt-out clause to escape social responsibility, but rather an invitation to use one's talents and skills to advance the cause of justice for all.

Like King, I get to call masses to a moment of action: to make decisions to lead, to confess, to celebrate, to reflect, and to make change. It is a humbling job and sometimes I wonder, How did I get to do this? How did I end up here? The lessons of leadership are in the journey. My journey to speak on stage didn't start and wasn't developed in front of the spotlight with applause or recognition. There was a process that was unseen, which led me to where I am today. The process included growing up in a faith community and seeing my mother speak with power and conviction on matters of faith, justice, and peace.

Events surrounding my childhood and being raised in an inner city were also part of the process. Years of set-backs and misfortunes as a young man in a household without a father, living in poverty, and witnessing domestic violence first-hand, were part of the process and development as a communicator. These, along with countless other experiences, moved me towards aspects of compassion, grace, redemption, community, and forgiveness. My ability to speak was shaped less by my skills and talents, but more by my heart-felt desire to hear and care for the needs of others. By God's grace, He has bestowed this gift upon me to advance my life through the teachings of the Scriptures and to summon the courage to live the life I was created to live on purpose.

Who are you trying to reach?

Do you have a strategy to communicate with others who are different from you?

What are you doing to be a more effective communicator?

THERE'S NOTHING ORDINARY
ABOUT EXTRAORDINARY

Sparkgood was founded on this simple idea: inviting people worldwide into choosing the extraordinary. Sparkgood provides coaching, workshops, and keynotes to help individuals and organizations choose the extraordinary. As a speaker, author, and social innovator, Jason continues to advance others forward to move beyond the barriers of things that are too common and comfortable. He ignites the spark to help you live more intentionally. Jason has worked with a number of organizations including Chick-Fil-A, Starbucks, The Style Network, and several colleges and universities around the world. He is one of my biggest cheerleaders and a journeyman who helped advance aspects of my personal and professional life in ways that are simply immeasurable. Jason models the extraordinary every day of his life. If you are in a room with him, you will quickly discover that you are in a unique space. You are in a room with a King Maker.

JASON JAGGARD
FOUNDER

SPARKGOOD

SPARKGOOD.COM

CHAPTER FOUR

THE POWER OF
ALIGNMENT

"The world changes not through declarations and legislation, but through the private conversations between key influencers."

– Marcus "Goodie" Goodloe, P.h.D.

CHAPTER 4

My first experience with a hammer occurred during the summer I was a pre-teen when I attempted to make money doing odd jobs. Robert, a childhood friend of the family, invited me to work with him in his lawn business. One particular day, we came across a yard that needed a number of project repairs. After carefully prioritizing, the first project we tackled was replacing a wooden structure that was used to house trash containers. I was charged with removing the wood planks and replacing the rusted nails. I was handed a tool that I did not have a clue how to use. I had seen others use one, so I mimicked the motions.

I proceeded to pound, knock, hit, slam, and nick at the wood planks. I mustered up enormous amounts of energy, only to discover I was exhausted and not making progress. Robert, who was by all accounts a professional, came alongside me. He placed his hands on my hand and began to hammer with me. All of a sudden, my aim for the actual nail improved, along with my pace and strength. I thought, *if I could have his hand on my hand doing all the work, this would be so much easier.* I never realized the skill required for hammering. It requires focus, alignment, control, and precision. I learned that if I needed more efficiency and power I had to swing from the elbow. It was all in the alignment. If I needed more control, I had to swing from the wrist. Robert taught me so much that summer about using the right tools for the right job– like a craftsman.

ONE MAN'S LOVE

When some people think about former President George W. Bush, they may think about the War in Iraq, "weapons of mass destruction," shoes being thrown in protest, or a "decider in chief." Others may think about 9/11, as he stood on a pile of rubble and said, "I can hear you." Those in Louisiana and the surrounding area may have visions of a flyover after hurricane Katrina when thousands were displaced as a result of one of the greatest natural disasters in our county's history. Others may recall Kanye West saying, "George Bush doesn't care about Black people" in response to the delayed aid for the residents in Louisiana. Still, others may recall over 6,000 troops killed during the wars in Afghanistan and Iraq, with tens of thousands injured, and thousands more suffering from post traumatic stress syndrome.

Whatever resonates with you on this list may pale in comparison to what this former President did to help others. In spite of all his leadership failures, George W. Bush was responsible for saving the lives of hundreds of thousands of people in developing countries. In fact, on March 17, 2002 the Bush Administration made history by announcing a five billion dollar foreign aid package. This effort surprised many humanitarian workers, activists, and politicians both foreign and domestic. [16]

The President's Emergency Plan for AIDS Relief (PEPFAR) remains the largest single commitment by any nation to address a single disease globally. In fact, during Bush's post-presidential years, he has continued to champion the fight against AIDS as well as other issues including economic growth, education reform, human freedom, and military service through the George W. Bush Institute.[17] Where did the idea for this historic piece of legislation come from? From pollsters? From politicians? How can we learn to create other movements like it?

Most people are unaware of the person responsible for bringing this opportunity to the President's attention, and thus will miss "Lesson 101" Of the Power of Alignment. Guess who was standing next to Bush during the press conference announcing this new initiative? It wasn't a politician. It wasn't a war vet or a native from a developing country. It wasn't his wife or daughters or any dignitary. It was a rock star. That's right. Positioned five feet from the most powerful man in the world, who was announcing the largest humanitarian effort in history, was a global celebrity. Donned in his iconic BVLGARI Italian sunglasses and trademark rogue black leather jacket was a man with only one name--Bono. It was Bono who advocated for debt relief in developing countries, the extensive promotion of education, and massive medical relief for AIDS and other diseases.[18] This is the result of the power of alignment and influence.

How did *that* happen? It was very simple: *Bono set up a meeting*. Not with the President. Not with the Vice President, but with a long-time senator by the name of Jesse Helms; a man who fought *against* nearly every piece of civil rights legislation in the last 50 years. The same man who had fought against commemorating a national holiday in honor of Dr. Martin Luther King Jr. Bono set up a meeting, and after that meeting, Jesse Helms spoke with Dick Cheney. President Bush told the story at the press conference, "Dick walked into my office and said, 'Jesse Helms wants you to meet with Bono.'" So the most powerful man in the world accepted a meeting with a rock star that changed the destiny of hundreds of thousands of Africans. It's not rocket science. It's leadership. It's the power of alignment.

> "One man come in the name of love
> One man come and go
> One man come he to justify
> One man to overthrow..."
>
> – Pride (In the Name of Love), U2

Where did Bono learn how to do that? From the very man Jesse Helms fought against having a holiday named after. Who knew that an entertainer could affect real political change in the world? Martin Luther King Jr. knew first-hand. Bono learned how to lead from reading about King. Bono knowingly and intentionally leveraged his influence in a way that was pioneered by King. It was one private meeting between a rock star and a racist politician that led to debt relief, AIDS awareness, and education for a struggling continent. It was through a strategy of activism honed by King in the 50s and 60s that has led to some of the most significant and progressive change in the world's history.

> "Early morning, April four
> Shot rings out in the Memphis sky
> Free at last, they took your life
> They could not take your pride..."
>
> – Pride (In the Name of Love), U2

PILLARS AT THE INTERSECTION OF

FAITH, POLITICS AND CULTURE.

LISA SHARON HARPER

CHIEF CHURCH ENGAGEMENT OFFICER

SOJOURERS: FAITH IN ACTION FOR SOCIAL JUSTICE, WASHINGTON, D.C.

SOJO.NET

Sojourners is an international network of people committed to putting their faith in action to transform the world. Whether you are passionate about your community, politics, culture, and faith, you will find a life-changing assignment to your biblical call at Sojourners. You will work alongside others from all walks of life and ideological persuasions who share your same passions and interests. Check out Sojourners website as they are currently tackling important issues such as Immigration, Poverty, Women & Girls empowerment, Climate Change, and Peace and Nonviolence. The company publishes a monthly magazine of the same name which they describe as a voice and vision for social change. I was fortunate to meet Lisa Sharon Harper years ago at a faith and justice conference and I came away from our interaction with the belief that she is a true difference maker. I was wrong, she's so much more: A King Maker!

STRIDES AHEAD

> "What he said opened up a new way
> of thought for me."
>
> – Jesse Owens

In 1936, Jesse Owens won gold medals in the long jump, 100 Meters, 200 Meters, and the 4x100 Relay. He managed to break or equal nine Olympic Records and also set three world records that year.[19] It wasn't just that Jesse Owens was fast. It wasn't just that he was the first athlete to win four gold medals. It was the context of an African-American athlete defeating not just one contender, but the German competitors four times in Berlin during one of the darkest and most prejudiced regimes in the history of the world. His accomplishments were an affront to the Aryan Race Superiority Theory advocated by Hitler and spreading through Western Europe at that time.

> "In one week in the summer of 1936
> on the sacred soil of the
> Fatherland the master athlete
> humiliated the master race." [20]
>
> – Larry Schwartz

Owens returned from Berlin to a ticker-tape parade down 5th Avenue in New York City, but he had to ride a "Coloreds Only" freight elevator in the Waldorf-Astoria Hotel to come out of the main entry to the parade. He was never acknowledged by President Roosevelt. He was not invited to the White House, nor was he given a letter of congratulations by the President. In fact, a few years after the 1936 Berlin Olympic Games, Jesse Owens fell on hard times. He faced financial troubles with the United States government and had to file for bankruptcy. To his embarrassment, one of the ways this decorated Olympic Medalist and national hero made money was running against horses in front of mostly white audiences. Due to these struggles, Owens was conflicted with the idea of being an African-American in a nation that celebrated his accomplishments on the track field, but rejected him at lunch counters.

Years later, a discouraged Owens crossed paths with King in a New York airport after a rally. They had a conversation that struck a chord with Owens. King discussed the idea of leveraging his power and fame as an athlete to advocate for civil rights and human equality. King urged the four gold medal winner to find a part of his life that was larger, yet related to his former experience as a world-class athlete.

Owens reflected on his encounter with King and wrote, "Martin helped me through that most difficult time. I'm not saying we were closest of friends. You didn't have to be close to Martin to have him hit you where you lived. . . . But what he said opened up a new way of thought for me." [21]

This story gives insight into one of King's greatest leadership legacies and a leader's greatest tool. Not only

influence than others because of wealth, status, or celebrity, and great leaders unashamedly step into this dynamic to bring about change in the world.

CONTINUOUS ALIGNMENT

In 1966, the great actor Marlon Brando was the focus of harsh criticism because he was unable to join a civil rights rally in Cambridge, Massachusetts, due to his ailing health. King came to his defense, not by making a speech or writing an Op-ed in The New York Times, but by writing a personal letter to Brando. King drew a correlation to his experience as a civil rights leader and being unfairly criticized, especially by good people who were simply unaware of all the facts:

> I remember well how you were the first to respond to Harry [Belafonte]'s request for assistance when I was being tried for perjury in Alabama several years ago. I also remember your great expression of support that you gave our movement when I last saw you in California. You can rest assured that your appearance on the front lines of the struggle for civil rights, whether in Cambridge, Maryland or elsewhere, is welcomed and gives great encouragement to all persons involved. [22]

King concluded his comments to Brando and stated that he was "eternally indebted" to the actor for his moral and financial support and his "genuine good will and unswerving devotion" to the movement. [23] In this moment of kindness, it wasn't a symbolic gesture but a simple, heartfelt letter. King connected to Brando as a fellow human being, which fostered the relationship between the two.

Likewise, when Sammy Davis, Jr., canceled as the headliner for a SCLC fundraiser due to an injury, King went to great lengths to express his appreciation to Davis for his time and consideration in desiring to be part of the event. Davis' response reflected the intimacy he and King shared. Sent by his manager, Davis' note read:

> *"Sammy sends his assurances to Dr. King that he will perform on behalf of SCLC sometime in the fall; however, doctor's [sic] desires that he not engage in anything outside of theatre currently prevents him from naming a specific date at this time. As soon as doctor sees fit to release him he will forward a confirmed date at once."* [24]

King did not leave the response of Davis' cancellation to an assistant or intermediary. Instead, he responded to Davis directly and spoke of the larger impact of the performer's life and legacy upon the movement. In a two page letter addressed to Davis, King encouraged him to get well and recover from his injury. He spoke in praise and adoration of Davis for his talents and skills, as well as the hope and anticipation people felt as a result of his coming. King wrote in future tense, as if it was not a matter whether Davis would come, but simply how soon:

> *"Please know that I greatly understand why it was necessary for you to postpone your engagement with us on July 25th. I am much more concerned about your health and welfare than about the benefit that your presence on that date would have brought to Atlanta."* [25]

King continued by discussing how Davis' visit would attract a cultural and ethnic audience consistent with the civil rights leader's dream for the nation: "I do hope, however, that it will be possible for you to do the benefit in

October or November," King wrote. "I would not even seek to persuade you to come at the time if I did not feel that your presence in Atlanta would serve as both a cultural and humanitarian purpose." [26] King informed Davis that he did not have to prove his commitment to the civil rights struggle or his allegiance to King. King concluded by writing, "I can assure you that SCLC could not make it without friends like you, and neither could I." [27]

Actor and television host Steve Allen faced criticism from his viewers for his support of King. One viewer accused Allen and King of being communists. That same guy further stated that Allen was misguided for his support of King and the Civil Rights Movement. Allen stood his ground and offered King the services of his personal attorney if the civil rights leader wanted to launch a formal defense against such slander. [28]

The personal relationships and influence King had with a handful of entertainers were significant and demonstrated his leadership and understanding of human nature. Actress and dancer Josephine Baker and King maintained a relationship based upon more than financial transactions and social status. Scholars have noted that, as in the case with Brando and Davis, King interfaced with Baker on a range of issues.

In one instance, after having reflected upon the March on Washington in 1963 in which she was honored to take part, Baker wrote to King:

"I was so happy to have been unified with all of you on our great historical day. I repeat that you are really a great, great leader and if you need me I will always be at your disposition because we have come a long way

but still have a way to go that will take unity—so don't forget I will always be one of your sincere boosters."[29]

King responded to Baker in kind:

"I am deeply moved by the fact that you would fly such a long distance to participate in that momentous event. We were further inspired that you returned to the States to do a benefit concert for the Civil Rights Organizations... Your genuine good will, your deep humanitarian concern, and your unswerving devotion to the cause of freedom and human dignity will remain an inspiration to generations yet unborn." [30]

King also showed compassion for athletes and entertainers which fostered healthy measures of communication. Singer Mahalia Jackson was in a billing dispute with a dentist who treated her after she made a joint appearance with King. SCLC and King believed the service was complimentary. King assigned Wyatt T. Walker, then Executive Director of SCLC, to resolve the matter.[31]

Think about it. Is there anything less exotic than helping a friend resolve a billing issue with a dentist? This is what friends do for each other. This is what parents do for their kids. It is a simple act of care that makes all the difference in the world to others. Writing letters of appreciation or using his resources to aid friends were other methods King used to serve people of great power and position. He treated them as regular people.

Think about this:

Who are the people of influence you know and what are their needs? Most of the time they are spiritual or relational needs.

Do they desire legitimate friendships?

Do they desire to do something for a lasting legacy?

How could you play a loving role in the life of those of influence? Not to get something from them, but simply to be a blessing.

• • •

> "I learned how to treat famous people from Dr. King. He modeled what it looked like to walk alongside people with amazing influence and serve them rather than judge or even push them away."
>
> – Marcus "Goodie" Goodloe, Ph.D.

Treating celebrities as people has been a major theme in my life as well. Several years ago a married couple I knew was on the hit show "Dancing with the Stars," which was ABC's number one rated show on television at that time. They began attending a church where I was working and we quickly became friends. One of the challenges they faced was how to be deeply involved in the entertainment industry and live out their faith in ways that were healthy and life-giving. They were gone so often and their work wasn't typical – like most people who work in a classroom, cubicle, or office. Instead, their workplace was a dance floor taping at a network television studio.

Over time we began a series of conversations which led to creative ways to invest in themselves and their industry friends. My wife Lucy and I, along with church volunteers, rented out restaurants in Manhattan Beach, California to host dinners where their friends of affluence could have Q&A's around spirituality. We provided them with encouraging books, podcasts, and other resources to nurture their faith. We worked with them on how to serve those in their community and invest in others spiritually, especially people of influence to whom they were being introduced. Our friends looked to us to teach them how to invest in people whom many of us would never meet. Most people of faith would typically write these celebrities off as uninterested in God. Yet with our support, and their strong desire to share their faith, our friends were now spending extensive hours working and traveling with people of great influence across the country. Regardless of pedigree, always keep in mind that we are all created in the image of God, and seek counsel to know if God is real, and can be trusted with our lives.

So let me ask you: *What meetings do you need to set up?*

My guess is that right now there's a meeting you could schedule that would move your cause, your idea, or your dream forward. Maybe it's with a person of influence. Maybe it's with your boss or with an employee or with a potential volunteer. Maybe it's with a friend or spouse. I don't know who it is, but you have dreams and ideas in your head that need to be born. The birthing process begins when you set up that first meeting to be in alignment with God and in alignment with someone to help you bring your idea to fruition.

CHAPTER FIVE

THE POWER OF
KNOWLEDGE

"Today, knowledge has power. It controls access to opportunity and advancement."

– Peter Drucker

CHAPTER 5

Education has played role in my upbringing. My mother, oldest sister, and godmother are educators. My life and worldview were shaped in large part by their investment in me, as well my observations of them serving the needs of others within their schools. I was fortunate to attend one of the best public universities in the country, The University of New Mexico, in Albuquerque, New Mexico, and eventually further my studies in two private institutions: Golden Gate Seminary, in San Francisco, and Dallas Baptist University, in Dallas, Texas. I have been humbled by the opportunity to serve over the last few years as an adjunct professor at my graduate and postgraduate schools. This type of service has truly been one of the joys of my life. I love the classroom.

When I consider the years spent on campus attending classes as a student, I can honestly say it was what I learned and experienced outside of my formal teaching settings that has been the most impactful. Lessons of sacrifice, commitment, trust, and overcoming the fear of failure in learning something new are just a few that come to mind. Additionally, some of the most significant relationships in my life emerged from my college interactions.

June 1986. Boy was I excited. My junior high graduation day had finally come. Now came the time for me to shine like the dawn. I remember feeling the thrill of achievement in passing all my classes so that I could attend Centennial High, in Compton, California. I beamed at the prospect of all the gifts I would receive as a result of this major accomplishment.

Rita Hayes, a deputy sheriff and my mother's close friend, brought me a huge professionally wrapped box which I just knew contained something cool, hip, and tailor-made for me. Ugh! Was I ever wrong! As I recall, some of my friends received wads of cash, video game consoles and accessories, skateboards, and clothes. I figured my odds of having at least one of these cool items in such a large box were definitely in my favor.

As I opened the wrapping paper, I discovered very quickly that I had a talent for acting. I remember saying to myself, Look happy, Goodie, look happy. But happiness was the furthest emotion I could think of. Instead, I was confused and disappointed. Why? Enclosed within that elegant wrapping paper were not one, but two books! That's right, two books that were well over one-thousand pages each! Not the latest CD or Atari video game or a pile of money, but two books! What was with this lady? One book was a dictionary. The other was a Bible. In the graduation card, she simply wrote, "These two books are the tools that will change your life. They will empower you." The Bible was one of the most powerful tools that carried King throughout his career. That experience has stayed with me for over 30 years, and I have been empowered by both of these tools. One gives me the ability to know the meaning of words; the other has given me the meaning of life itself. Talk about empowering!

> "Education must enable one to sift and weigh evidence, to discern the true from the false, the real from the unreal, and the facts from the fiction. The function of education, therefore, is to teach one to think intensively and to think critically. But education which stops with efficiency may prove the greatest menace to society...
>
> – Dr. Martin Luther King, Jr.

Education was a key tool that King utilized in order to advance his ideas. The excerpt above was taken from a speech he gave to the United Federation of Teachers in 1947. While at Morehouse College, King also wrote a column in the campus paper titled, "The Purpose of Education." Education is one of the best ways to advance cultures and empower individuals to dream and work toward a better future.

King's desire to intertwine theology with social action was birthed after graduating from Morehouse College, in Georgia. He credits Benjamin Mays as his spiritual advisor during his studies at Crozer Theological Seminary in Pennsylvania where he graduated as valedictorian. King continued his education and earned his Ph.D. from Boston

University at the age of 25. It was when he was working on his dissertation that he met his wife, Coretta Scott, who was studying voice and piano. King married Coretta a few years later and they had four children. Mrs. Coretta Scott-King was an advocate for civil rights and worked side-by-side with her husband and carried the torch until her death in 2006.

King read Plato, Aristotle, Luther, Locke, Kant, and Rousseau. He was constantly searching for the truth in history and was influenced by Hegel and Marx. He became a follower of Gandhi's nonviolent movement and studied Walter Rauschenbusch's work on the church being socially responsible for seeking justice. In addition, King read history: American, Jewish, ancient, and that of various cultures to frame his philosophical viewpoints and advance his ideas for social reform.

King's keen awareness of Biblical history also aided him in calling out blatant wrongs of society. He wanted to bring attention to the large majority of white cultural Christians who participated in the unfair and unjust treatment of African-Americans, dating back to the birth of the nation. King classified these individuals as "children of darkness." He believed that those who perpetrated hatred seemed to be more determined to create division over Christians, whom he termed "children of light." He called on Christians to do more. Dr. King believed that God's heart was for justice, and it was up to us to care for the poor and underrepresented as expressed in the Scriptures. He often quoted from the Bible to educate his audience about taking up their crosses for social reform. [32]

Throughout his short life, King used his knowledge

and skills to birth other leaders. He was trained to lead and was now shaping young leaders. King was bothered by the discrepancies in the educational system. How can one lead without the knowledge and tools to do so? He wanted an educational system where every child received a true education to prepare him or her for the future.

In examining King's life, I learned that he was much more than a learned man in formal disciplines such as reading, writing, and arithmetic. Instead, King was a learner of people and the context and times in which he lived. Upon his arrival in Montgomery, Alabama, King became a student of the city, particularly in aspects of economics, as well as the social and political landscapes. He noted disparities between African-Americans and whites in levels of income, as well as challenges on matters such as fair and equal access to public housing. He recognized the inadequate transportation in the poorest neighborhoods in comparison to the most affluent, and he saw the lack of opportunities people of color struggled with because they did not live in close proximity to basic, daily necessities like local drug and grocery stores.

King was committed to educating local congregations and building interfaith alliances across denominational lines. The track record of organizations mounting collective efforts in confronting racism and injustice was average in Montgomery prior to King's arrival. King spoke of the necessity of African-Americans to working with whites. He strengthened his involvement with the National Baptist Convention, which at the time was one of the nation's largest and predominantly African-American organizations. King joined committees, attended annual meetings, and thrust himself into the Baptist preaching circles of white and African-American alike. He did not want African-Americans to have an "excess of skepticism" toward whites, because he desired for both races to join their abilities and enter into committed partnerships in bringing respect and dignity to all citizens.

King's knowledge and understanding of the struggle and heartache that many African-Americans faced in the cities and nation as a whole was second to none. His classroom was the human soul; King read the hearts and minds of people with vigor and vitality. With an educator's passion and persistence, he was committed to bringing others along to pass the test presented before the nation: to indeed become one nation, under God, indivisible, with liberty and justice for all. This was the power and presence King had as a leader. His influence and willingness to learn from others knew no limits: the small farmer, blue collar worker, garment district vendor, sanitation worker, the priest, Rabbi, the political activist, the local city's elected town clerk, the nation's highest appointed judges, and most certainly, athletes and entertainers were a natural part of his cohort.

When King decided to take a formal position in opposition to President Johnson and his administration's policy in Vietnam, the civil rights leader solicited the help of actors and activists Dick Gregory and Harry Belafonte. King knew of their involvement in protesting the country's escalating involvement in Southeast Asia, and he wanted to gain insights from two people who were already engaged in the struggle to end the nation's fighting on foreign soil. King asked Belafonte to conduct an extensive study on the subject, collect relevant facts and information on Vietnam and the nation's policy, and provide a profile of its noted political history, including its leaders Ho Chi Minh and Ngo Dinh Diem. Belafonte stated that King was a student, and he desired those closest to him to do their "homework" on the subject of Vietnam; the heart of King's "coalition of conscience" was at stake. "Dr. King clearly felt that on the issue of Vietnam," Belafonte stated, "he was going to be standing way, way alone. He spent several years trying to get people unified; no single act would insure disunity as much as the Vietnam thing."[33]

The Power of Knowledge.

King included educational materials in mail packets to athletes and entertainers in order to keep them informed of the latest initiatives and campaigns by the SCLC. It was not enough for athletes and entertainers to know who King was; the civil rights leader wanted them to know about the movement and how the organization he led was committed to advancing matters of justice and peace.

As the leader of the SCLC, King had the personal touch. He knew it was important to develop and maintain substantive relationships. King wanted athletes and entertainers to know their financial contributions were important to the movement, and that every dollar given or pledged to the Civil Rights Movement made a difference to advance the cause of justice and freedom across the South, and the nation. King made a point to personally sign thank you correspondence to athletes and entertainers who gave money to the movement. Actor Burt Lancaster gave to the SCLC and supported King. For his contribution of $1,000, King informed him that his gift allowed for the SCLC to continue the quest to "redeem the soul of America." In a letter to actress and dancer Eartha Kitt, King acknowledged her artistic contributions to society and thanked her for her financial support of the Civil Rights Movement. Kitt gave $1,000, and in her letter accompanying her contribution she wrote, "I hope it makes the way a little easier for the thing we all want in this beautiful but disturbed country."[34]

The Power of Knowledge.

King used the media to keep athletes and entertainers informed, as well as the broader public, as to the message and mission of civil rights. He knew the importance of not only staying on message, but getting his message out. King made urgent appeals to local and national newspapers for people to support the cause of the SCLC and the Civil Rights Movement. King gave interviews and wrote editorials to some of the nation's leading papers and television programs, including the New York Times, Time, Washington Post, Chicago Tribune, Los Angeles Times, CBS's "Face the Nation," and NBC's "Meet the Press." And here's a point of note: Well-wishers from the entertainment community and athletic fields learned of King and the movement through such mediums before they actually met him in person. People sent telegrams and letters of affirmation to King, partly due to exposure from the national media.

The nation's television networks and news outlets covered King's speech, "Give Us the Ballot," which he delivered at the Prayer Pilgrimage on May 17, 1957. One of the onlookers via television was baseball great Jackie Robinson. After seeing King and reading about the march in the national news in 1957, he sent a contribution to the SCLC addressed to the young leader. King responded by offering a special thanks to Robinson. Robinson replied,

"No thanks needed Dr. King. It was the least I could do as a result of the benefits afforded to me by your efforts and sacrifice of organizations like the NAACP and SCLC."[35]

Knowledge is more than information. Having all the facts or being aware of the problems is only half of the equation. For leaders to advance and move others along with them more is needed. Leaders must be willing to act on the information and knowledge they obtain.

Billy Sanderson is one of the closest people to me on planet Earth. He and his wife Michelle are amazing human beings. Billy and I met in Dallas when we served as youth pastors in local churches. I have talked to him about his brief time in the military and recently asked him about the term "actionable intelligence" or AI as it's referred to. I hear it used almost daily it seems and wanted to know more. In short, it is the idea that information gathered on the ground about hostiles or the enemy that is good enough to act upon, will place the good guys at an advantage. AI allows military personnel to gain the necessary background and details in order to accurately assess and implement a tactical strategy or strike. It's not enough to simply have an idea of where a target is located. That's only the first step. The question that remains is twofold: Can the information that has been obtained be acted upon? And, does one have the means and resources to execute a plan to move things forward?

King gave us a roadmap to follow. He was a student of the context and people around him; he invited others to share and speak into the issues he was committed to change. As the moral leader of his time, King used various mediums to engage and keep others informed, and King drew on the strength of the relationships around him in order to advance the Civil Rights Movement. He had a personal touch, and went out of his way to make sure athletes and entertainers knew their sacrifice of time and money was not in vain. There were things King did not know. But, there were people he knew who knew those things he needed to know; King lead and served them accordingly. He obtained relevant and pertinent information to the mission he was called to lead, and proceeded to move forward with a plan.

King was the master at gaining knowledge and insight as to what needed to be done. His ability to assess conditions around him and implement the necessary strategies and tactics for success was nothing short of brilliant. He had a well informed gift of identifying key individuals and groups who would be needed to advance the message that the nation needed to hear: No longer was it acceptable to have two Americas where one group of people were mistreated based solely on the basis of the color of their skin.

TRAIN UP
A CHILD
TO LEAD

If you want to change leaders, focus on them when they are young." The Nelsons have spent decades growing great leaders. They have created a revolutionary curricula, LeadYoung, that focuses on training 16 character and competency skills that separate great leaders from the rest. The leadership programs are age-specific, and are designed for kids and young adults ages 2-25. KidLead believes that targeting leaders while they are young and moldable will develop exceptional leaders in the future. Dr. Alan Nelson is regarded as a global leadership expert in young leader development. He has authored 20 books and published more than 200 feature articles on leadership topics. His wife, Nancy, served as the junior high director alongside John Maxwell, the #1 leadership expert in the world. The Nelsons have embodied King Maker leadership characteristics with their own three sons, and are passionate about empowering generations of King Makers for years to come.

DR. ALAN NELSON + NANCY NELSON

CO-FOUNDERS

KID LEAD

KIDLEAD.COM

CHAPTER SIX

THE POWER OF
COMMITMENT

KNOWING YOUR TRUE NORTH

"Everything can't be important or nothing is important."
– Marcus "Goodie" Goodloe, Ph.D.

CHAPTER 6

For an extended period of my life I served as a youth pastor. One year, while serving in Dallas, Texas, I traveled with youth and adult volunteers to a camp called Kids Across America, in Missouri. Spending a hot summer on a bus for an eight-hour ride was certainly not my idea of summer vacation. I still remember the mantra of the camp. It was simple, yet served as a powerful reminder for what it means to live a life committed to serving others: "God first, others second, and I'm third." In other words, it's not about you!

My primary charge was to help youth reach their fullest redemptive potential and to live out the life God created for them. There is a passage of Scripture that served as the central focus for every youth ministry position I held: "And Jesus grew in wisdom and in favor with God and others" (36). This passage of Scriptures speaks to me in so many different ways. For one, it reminds me of what my priorities were then and what they are now, in helping to move people forward in faith. Additionally, it points to the need and constant thirst we must have to grow and develop in various aspects of our lives. So often we grow in one area of our life, while we neglect others. We grow in physical health, but fail to stretch our minds; or, we grow in relationships with others, but fail to understand who we are or to discover our unique gifts and talents. As a result, self-learning and development takes a back seat.

When I consider King's life and legacy, and, most

importantly, his leadership with athletes and entertainers during the Civil Rights Movement, it is obvious that he lived his life for the benefit of others. He was totally committed. He grew and formed deep and meaningful relationships with others, which made them walk even closer with him. These relationships helped him gain clarity on who he was and how he was created, which gave him a greater appreciation for the gifts and talents given to him by God.

Early in his public ministry, King's commitment and view of coalition-building were put to the test. Within a year, King was thrust onto the national stage when he became president of the Montgomery Improvement Association (MIA), an organization whose origins stemmed from the segregation policy on its public transportation system.

On December 1, 1955, Rosa Parks, a local seamstress and member of the NAACP, refused to give up her seat on a bus. She was arrested, jailed, and fined for her actions. Activist E. D. Nixon, a local railroad porter, was called. Nixon then called two other activists, Fred Gray and Virginia Durr. The three decided that they would assist Parks by fighting against the discriminatory charges. Parks thanked them and replied, "If you think it will mean something to Montgomery, I'll be happy to go along with it."[37]

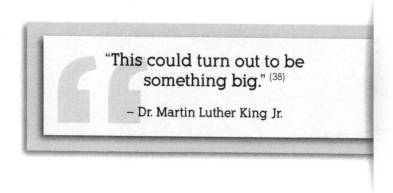

"This could turn out to be something big." [38]

– Dr. Martin Luther King Jr.

Nixon called on King, the Reverend Ralph Abernathy, and other civil rights leaders to confront the unfair Montgomery busing policy that violated the rights of Blacks. At Alabama State, King and the other activists made copies of leaflets that pointed out Montgomery's discrimination against Blacks and described Ms. Parks' situation, then distributed them throughout local churches. King rushed home to gain his wife's support in his new role as activist and to prepare his remarks.

When he arrived at the church, it took several minutes for him to find his way through the crowd waiting in line outside. Thousands continued to flood the already filled balconies and aisles inside. It was clear that the thousands who gathered to protest the policies by the Montgomery city officials were determined to bring about change. King made his way to the pulpit at Holt Street Baptist Church to give his first speech, which he later deemed as the most decisive speech of his life. The protest movement was only one day old, and King let everyone know on that day that he was committed to the cause of African-Americans as well as causes for all humanity.

• • •

FOREVER FAMILY
FOR EVERY CHILD

ALAIN J. DATCHER

CHILD WELFARE ADVOCATE.

/ALAIN.DATCHER

Alain is a passionate advocate for the foster care system because it was his lifeline to success. "If it had not been for the foster care system, I would not be alive today. I was headed on the path of the all too common statistic: drug dealer, gang member or deceased." A native of Inglewood, Alain was placed in the system at an early age. As a college student at Biola University, he was selected as a Capitol Hill intern to provide a much needed voice for changing the adoptive and foster care policies. I first met Alain at Pepperdine University, in Malibu, California while I was guest speaker for the Martin Luther King Jr. Chapel and Celebration. From his command of the stage and presence, I knew he was someone I had to meet. We had lunch two weeks later and I learned of his amazing journey: "Like King, I also have a dream; to see every child in this country in a permanent, safe, loving home." Alain travels across the United States speaking and advocating on issues of foster care and adoption, and community development. King would be proud of this young King

King was committed to being a voice for all people regardless of race, creed, or color. In 1965, he stood in oppotsition to President Lyndon Johnson's policy in Southeast Asia and called for a complete withdrawal and curtailment of sending American Marines to Vietnam. During a speech at Howard University, King said that the war was "accomplishing nothing." His remarks caused problems for many athletes and entertainers who were contributors to his success and supporters of his efforts. Not only that, but other organizations were torn on how to deal with the evolution of King's activism. Leaders of the two most respected civil rights organizations in the world—the NAACP and the SCLC—maintained a constant feud. In addition to philosophical differences, neither of them agreed to the tactics for moving forward and how to solicit and maintain finances. Whites, as well as African-Americans, blamed King for violence and accused him of being an agitator and an outsider.

As a result of King's criticism of the Johnson administration, members of the SCLC board distanced themselves from King's actions in fear of economic collapse. Arguments broke out over who would speak on behalf of the interest and future of African-Americans in public settings. Fellow African-American leaders accused King of being a media hog. In one instance, King's closest confidant and lawyer, Clarence Jones, asked Belafonte to moderate a truce meeting with members of SNCC.

Clergy members, civil rights leaders, and members of Congress admonished King to stick to the business of civil rights. As with the Black Power debate, athletes and entertainers shared a fraction of the national stage with King on the issues of war and peace. Muhammad Ali, Eartha

Kitt, Ossie Davis, Harry Belafonte, Dick Gregory, and Joan Baez were among those who supported King. Additionally, Jackie Robinson and Jesse Owens believed King's position and condemnation were un-American at the very least and unwise at best. The criticism King faced influenced and brought challenges in dealing with athletes and entertainers.

Yet for King, his increased focus on the war wasn't a departure from his previous mission but rather an extension of it. King sought to internationalize the ideals of America, including democracy, freedom, and equality, and thereby to measure not only its domestic policies, but also the country's foreign policy by these same ideals. This forced prominent individuals, who used their celebrity status to advance the civil rights agenda, to evaluate the sincerity of their convictions for supporting King in one of the nation's most divisive issues.

So, what do you do when people begin to attack you? What do you do when you want something that might be controversial? What do you do when you're choosing something that is proving to be unpopular at best and potentially damaging at worst? What do you do when you want to do something that brings light to darkness, wholeness to brokenness, even though it might be controversial?

King had to find an internal space that made his efforts meaningful. Fortunately, he found what leadership expert Steven Covey describes as his "True North" [39]. King reflected and evaluated how his current actions were congruent with who he was as a man, an activist, and a child of God. This reflection took on the form of a list. He made a list of convictions and a list of values. With regard to his beliefs about Vietnam, he developed seven reasons why the U.S. should not be involved, with each point nestled in his overarching stance as a pacifist.

First, King believed the war took the focus off of the Great Society, a series of social programs designed to provide a better future for the nation's poor. The war was an enemy of the poor, which exploited the least and those marginalized in the United States and Vietnam. [40] Second, King argued that African-Americans were being drafted in disproportionate numbers to whites; the casualty rate was unacceptable.[41] Third, King believed that fighting for the rights of the South Vietnamese, while failing to have normal rights of decency in America, was internally wrong. King argued that forming an alliance with the peace movement protest would embolden the Civil Rights Movement.

A fourth reason King objected to the war was he felt his award of the Nobel Peace Prize was an international commission given to him to represent the interests of the global community, not simply the interests of the United States. Fifth, King believed his critique of the war was consistent with the mission statement of the SCLC: "to save the soul of America." Additionally, King stated that the future of the nation weighed in the balance with respect to its policy toward Vietnam. Finally, King was first and foremost a preacher, and his obligation to God involved representing the weak and those who suffered at the hands of the powerful. [42]

King's philosophical and religious stance on the Vietnam War ruffled a lot of feathers on both sides, yet his commitment was unwavering. Having a firm commitment is the first step in finding your true north. It is the deep reflection of one's self to discover what you believe, what is important to you, and how to live those ideals out in concrete, measurable ways. This is exactly what King did. He remained focused on what Cornell West referred to as a "prophetic Christian lens" to examine how far the nation had strayed from its democratic and humane ideals.[43] Even when people disagreed or were threatened by this viewpoint, it remained a guiding focus for his life and leadership.

A refrain I use often that has become a principle I live by is simply this: "Everything can't be important or nothing is important." There have been far too many times where I could not achieve optimal goals and objectives for my life because, quite frankly, everything seemed to possess the same amount of importance and commitment. When this happened to me as it does inevitably to each of us, we expend energy and make the meaningful things meaningless and we make the meaningless things meaningful. Both cannot be realities in our lives. Therefore, what has helped me remain focused is to make a list of priorities with deadlines to achieve them.

Another step in finding your True North involves looking for allies. It is always good to go back and revisit those people and experiences that demonstrated the full expression of what and who you were committed to. Garnering new friends for support can also be rewarding. For King, this meant finding an unlikely ally in the midst of his growing beliefs: Muhammad Ali. The heavyweight fighter rejected King's invitation to join the Civil Rights Movement years earlier. Yet by the height of the Vietnam War, they found a common ground—one based upon moral protest. On March 29, 1967, Ali met with King. He informed the heavyweight champion of possible consequences, including loss of his title and incarceration, if he refused to register for the draft. Ali and

King conducted a joint press interview. King stated that, although they had different religious beliefs, he and Ali had common problems and concerns regarding the Vietnam War.

> "Ali had something I have never been able to attain and something very few people I know possess. He had an absolute sincere faith." [44]
>
> –Bill Russell

Prominent athletes asked Ali not to join King and take on the Johnson administration, nor to have the nation question his patriotism for his refusal to register for the draft. The Boston Celtics' Bill Russell, Cleveland Browns' Jim Brown, and legendary UCLA Coach John Wooden attempted to advise Ali to change his position. Ali was criticized, and members of the media questioned the sincerity of his reasons for protest. The ten-member, high-powered delegation committed to persuade Ali to forgo his protest failed in its quest. Russell supported Ali's right to protest, but feared the consequences of his courage were too much for one man to bear during such a sensitive time.

Ali embraced political radicalism under the banner of his conversion to Islam. He exchanged correspondences with King in relation to the government's decision to prosecute him for his stance involving the war. King continued to advise Ali and offered "moral support and words of encouragement." Ali's public stance took on a greater impact, as most who opposed the war did so with the base and support of an organization or group. Ali was not afraid to stand on his own. He was the heavyweight champion of the world--not a candidate running for office. He did not need any type of corporate support or sponsorship. His efforts embodied the frustrations of millions, and fostered protest movements on subjects ranging from war and peace to the Olympics.

STILL STANDING

As King's convictions grew, his alliances shrank. Yet he kept pressing forward. With meager support from his coalition of conscience, on April 4, 1967, at the Riverside Church in New York City, King did what he had never done before and what became a defining moment in his leadership legacy. With 3,000 people in attendance, including members of the press from dozens of television and print media outlets, King delivered a formal speech in opposition to the war. With bulbs flashing, cameras rolling, and reporters furiously scribbling, King stated that he could no longer be silent; if his truest assessment of the war remained muted, it would be a betrayal to the nation's troops, his global citizenship, and the civil rights campaign. By following his moral convictions, King knew it would be difficult to influence Johnson on poverty and the civil rights agenda. King accused the Johnson administration of promoting violence. He reiterated his sevenfold objection, urging people to object to the war and the nation's draft policy on the basis of conscience.

It was one of King's greatest moments of moral clarity and bravery. Yet King's speech drew immediate rebuke. Prominent civil rights organizations, media outlets, and some of the nation's most famous athletes were critical of King's remarks. The NAACP's entire sixty-member board passed a unanimous resolution and stated that the discussion of civil rights in connection with the Vietnam War was a tactical mistake. Whitney Young of the Urban League, Jackie Robinson, Senator Edward Brooke of Massachusetts (the first African-American senator since Reconstruction), the Jewish War Veterans of America, Ralph Bunch, and Jesse Owens all stated that King was not a military expert, that he had no right to make such comments and that anti-war protests and civil rights messages were separate issues. They joined Wilkins in stating that the civil rights agenda needed to be won on its own merits and not tied to the subject of war and peace.

Media outlets, including the *New York Times, Los Angeles Herald Examiner, and the Washington Post,* accused King of being irresponsible and unsupported by the facts. The SCLC, concerned about its funding and support from moderate whites, attempted to distance itself from King's speech at Riverside. Board members sent a letter to supporters stating that King's views did not represent the formal policy stance of the SCLC. King's close advisor, Stanley Levison, informed King that he would be accused of leading a fringe movement of government and that his decision to oppose Johnson's war policy would ruin him. Members of the SCLC board accused King of trying to force his views upon the organization's leadership, as a Catholic bishop would to local churches.

The divisions between King and Johnson's

administration widened after the Riverside speech despite public support from some of the nation's most visible athletes and entertainers, such as Ali, Baez, Kitt, and Belafonte. King became a primary political enemy to the Johnson administration and J. Edgar Hoover. President Johnson authorized the FBI director to conduct a smear campaign, with allegations of marital affairs and financial improprieties, and being sympathetic toward Communist principles.

King did not waiver. He canceled a meeting with President Johnson, and a few days later, he increased his criticism of the war. Belafonte joined King and participated in a United Nations anti-war march. James Bevel, close friend and advisor of King, organized a group called the Spring Mobilization to End the War in Vietnam (Spring Mobe). The protest represented the nation's first major attempt to build a coalition between peace activists and civil rights leaders. King and Belafonte joined over 100,000 people in New York City's Central Park to voice objections to the war. King's inner circle remained divided over King's involvement in the anti-war movement. Despite such criticisms all around him, King did not back down. This was a testament to his leadership.

• • •

As a young man, my True North was football. It was to provide the economic pathway out of the cycle of poverty I was born into. To this day, I do not like anything that comes in threes! There was never an abundance in my household. Life was difficult for me and my two sisters growing up. We were raised by my mother who worked multiple jobs to make ends meet. When I was being recruited in high school to play football at the college level, I was only one of thousands and I remember wanting to go to UCLA. They were interested in me, but they didn't think I could handle the academic rigor of the school and did not offer me a scholarship. I remember being extremely disappointed.

Instead of wallowing in that disappointment, I chose to view my situation with a critical eye and realized that I had not achieved my optimal levels of performance on the field or in the classroom. So I kept pushing forward, and other schools pursued me. I found myself on a college campus at the University of New Mexico with a full scholarship. The year I graduated high school I was in the top 20 quarterbacks in the state – one of two African- Americans in the state to receive that honor.

Through a series of medical exams the coaches became nervous about the physical condition of my heart so I was benched before the season started. I remember hitting the wall of fear and doubt and once again dealing with obstacles to what I felt I was supposed to be doing in that season of my life. I remember lying in the University of New Mexico Hospital undergoing thousands of dollars of testing. Those became some of the darkest moments of my life.

From the time I was a teenager, I remember Dr. King having said that it's only when it's darkest that you can see the stars. I think your True North is found most in the darkness, in moments of adversity and trial. Whether it's a school saying they don't think you can cut the mustard or a physical ailment sidelining you, or in King's case, people of power saying you're off track or friends bailing on you, you have to push ahead. It's in those seasons you're challenged to ask the question, "Do I really believe in this?"

For me, finding my True North was about recommitting to what I was all about – playing football at the college level and getting a world class education. So I hired a tutor, took practice tests, and kept my grades up. Even though I couldn't play, I kept going to practice and team meetings, learned the plays, spent time with the other quarterbacks and coaches, and watched film. Despite having a medical disengagement, I found a way to engage in the sport and program to the best of my abilities. I was determined to find my True North and do whatever was necessary in the face of overwhelming obstacles to stay the course. I believed in me.

Finally, finding your True North – finding your stars in the darkness – is ultimately about finding the God who is the Creator of those stars. It's about knowing God's plan for your life and discovering what your purpose is while you are here on earth. It's about finding out what you were born to do.

On February 4, 1968, just months before King was assassinated, he told people what he wanted on his obituary:

If any of you are around when I have to meet my maker, I don't want a long funeral. And if you get somebody to deliver the eulogy, tell him not to talk too long. Every now and then I wonder what I want him to say, tell him not to mention that I have a Nobel Peace Prize, that isn't important. Tell him not to mention that I have 300 or 400 other awards, that's not important. Tell him not to mention where I went to school. I'd like somebody to mention that day when Martin Luther King Jr. tried to give his life serving others. I'd like for somebody to say that day that Martin Luther King Jr. tried to love somebody. I want you to say that day that I've tried to be right on the walk with them. I want you to be able to say that day that I did try to feed the hungry. I want you to be able to say that day I did try in my life to clothe all the naked.

UN*BEE*LIEVABLE!

THERE IS SWEETNESS IN HOPE

CHRISTOPHER CARLBERG

CEO

HALLELUJAH
HONEY

THANKTHELORDFORHONEY.COM

I've been fortunate to meet a lot of people from various walks of life and professions, as I travel the country speaking. But until 2015, I had never met a beekeeper. I met Christopher, an Environmental Scientist, at California Baptist University in Riverside, California, when I was invited to be the chapel speaker. Afterwards we grabbed lunch and I had a chance to meet his wife and beautiful family. Christopher has a passion to bring the goodness of taste to others without any additives or artificial ingredients. Before he was a beekeeper, Christopher was an exterminator– yes, a bee killer! He became a passionate lover of bees and what they offer to our environment, not to mention to our taste buds. As a beekeeper, Christopher spends his time harvesting honey and sharing the sweetness with others. His work is less about sales profits, and more about the community and conversations that are created around his passion. As a Kingmaker, he gives a percentage of the honey proceeds along with his time and energy to help advance a message of generosity, kindness, and love to those who desperately need it in a world of uncertainty and fear.

I want you to say on that day I did try in my life to visit those who were in prison. And I want you to say that I tried to love and serve humanity. Yes, if you want to say that I was a drum major. Say that I was a drum major for justice. Say I was a drum major for peace. I was a drum major for righteousness. And all of the other shallow things will not matter. [45]

King was committed to living his life influenced by the scriptures. The movement he led was a deep expression of his beliefs that everyone, regardless of their race, creed, or color, had the right to be free from injustice. King made decisions, even at the expense of his well-being and the well-being of his family, which placed others before him. The movement he led was never about him, but rather about the hope he had for humankind. [46]

Dr. King had this sense he was born to be a drum major. He was born to be a leader; however, he was born not only to lead, but to lead others towards justice, towards peace and love. That was his True North. It cost him friends, popularity, power, and ultimately his life. Yet, he found something worth giving his life for– leading others to see themselves in a more positive and powerful light.

So let me ask you, what's your True North?

What's in your life that's worth fighting for, that's worth giving your life to?

What is your sense of purpose?

What do you believe you have been created to do?

What must you do now because of that?

CHAPTER SEVEN

THE POWER OF
MONEY

"Leaders love what can be accomplished with money."

– Marcus "Goodie" Goodloe, Ph.D.

CHAPTER 7

This may sound obvious, but doing good in the world costs money– lots of it! Those who seek to make the world a better place must learn how to leverage money to accomplish their missions. Often when we think of movements we have this idea that they begin to take on a life of their own, that there's a critical tipping point where the wind fills the sails, the tide begins to change, and suddenly it becomes easy. Nothing could be further from the truth.

It is true that when people do the hard work, the impact of their work begins to grow exponentially. As leaders give 110%, they begin to see the results of their efforts grow more than they could ever imagine. So, it may seem that the leader has eased up his efforts; however, the secret of leadership is this: it never stops.

Whether it's women's suffrage, civil rights, the spiritual revivals of the early 19th and 20th centuries, or the environmental rights movement of the early 21st century, every movement is the result of prior years of tireless, relentless, and passionate work. I've found that one of the elements of work we tend not to think about, especially when it comes to non-profit or altruistic social movements, is the area of money.

Money is necessary in order to move forward and grow

any organization or cause; make no mistake about it. Asking others for money is one of the most critical tasks for leaders of faith-based organizations or grassroot movements. Like Dr. King, my leadership experiences often involved asking for money, which is challenging because money has become so idolized in our nation and around the world. Most people are reluctant to part with their cash because they are skeptical as to whether the leader will really use it for the benefit of the organization. One of the greatest and most humbling compliments I received was from a former senior pastor who said, "Goodie, people trust you with their money." Wow! As leaders, people are willing to give you what you need if they trust and believe in the cause and purpose which you are championing. Before you ask for money, make sure you have built a foundation of trust and mutual respect through relationship building.

Too often I meet spiritual leaders who are squeamish when it comes to asking for or talking about money. I meet people who accuse non-profits of speaking too much about money publicly. Some even try to sound spiritual while they're doing it, by quoting Scripture that says "the love of money is the root of all kinds of evil."[47]. Yes, that is true, and the same could be said about the fear of money.

Loving money leads to all kinds of evil. But good leaders love what can be accomplished with money. Let me say that again: leaders love what can be accomplished with money. They don't see a yacht or wrap-around porches in every dollar. Instead, they see a child in need of food, clothing, or shelter or a vital cause being funded. They unashamedly request resources from those who have it because they believe that money can be put toward the cause is better than money in their pockets. You show me a leader who is nervous about asking for money and I'll show you a leader who doesn't believe in what he/she is doing.

When I hit a wall during my doctoral research on Dr. King's leadership with athletes and entertainers, my professor and good friend Mike Williams told me, "Goodie, just follow the money!" Enthusiasm ensued. I purchased a plane ticket within days of that admonishment and found myself at the King Center in Atlanta focusing on such. Nearly half a dozen times or more, as I focused on the money, it became clear how money played a role in advancing the Civil Rights Movement. When it comes to the Civil Rights Movement, it is impossible to overemphasize the role that cash played in its success.

One of the most historic events that shaped the character of the nation and forced average citizens and political officials to reconsider their treatment of African-Americans was the Birmingham Campaign (or "Project C," which stood for Confrontation) in 1963. It was a testament to King's leadership with athletes and entertainers. King argued that the summer of 1963 was revolutionary because it changed the face of America. Freedom and the sacrifices necessary to achieve it became contagious. Birmingham served as an anchor point. That event highlighted King's abilities as a leader to influence some of the nation's most celebrated cultural and social icons. A shift occurred in the potential of the Civil Rights Movement and the impact it could have on the nation, not simply on the South. [48] Momentum was a measurable outcome of the Birmingham Campaign. Tangible results influenced by Project C included the passage of the Civil Rights Act of 1964 and 1965.

Many historians of American History noted that after the Birmingham Campaign, media attention grew, and the nation took notice of the movement as a whole because of Birmingham. Other scholars, including Michael Eric Dyson and Adam Fairclough, argue that the Birmingham campaign initiative and ultimate victory solidified King and the importance of the SCLC. [49] It brought awareness to opponents and proponents alike that the methods of nonviolent directed action could work. In addition, writer Donald T. Phillips contends that King developed "lofty" and "sweeping goals" for the movement during the Birmingham campaign, which allowed people to unite in their efforts to end poverty and prejudice and to bring fair play and equality to all Americans. [50]

BAIL MONEY

Perhaps the most controversial aspect of Project C (the Birmingham Movement) came in King's decision to invite young people to flood the jails alongside him in protest. The criticism of antagonists and sympathizers alike flourished in Birmingham. High school students were interviewed by King's staff and given leaflets and an orientation of what to expect when arrested. King needed support from his coalition-of-conscience citizens, including African-Americans who were apathetic and reluctant to get involved. King believed student involvement would bring a dramatic dimension to the campaign. King wrote:

> Our people were demonstrating daily and going to jail in numbers, but we were still beating our heads against the brick wall of the city officials' stubborn resolve to maintain the status quo. Our fight, if won, would benefit people of all ages. But most of all we were inspired with the desire to give to our young a true sense of their own stake in freedom and justice. We believed they would have the courage to respond to our call. [51]

Now, you might be asking, how does a boycott cost money? By definition, a boycott is where you don't spend money. Indeed, the goal of the Birmingham campaign was to wage an economic protest against businesses and store owners during the high shopping season of Easter. However, the protests resulted in the arrest of the protesters, and if they could not make bail, King ran the risk of hundreds of people suffering indefinite imprisonment. This meant those people in jail would not only be stuck in jail, but they could not work to support their families, let alone help fund the Civil Rights Movement, which was poorly funded to begin with.

On March 31, 1963, Belafonte hosted a meeting at his New York apartment with some of the movement's most vibrant supporters. He informed King that it would be wise to include entertainers and athletes in the planning of the protest and to allow them to give input, to which King agreed. All seventy-five people who attended the meeting at Belafonte's apartment were sworn to secrecy. King and Fred Shuttlesworth spoke in stark terms of the dangers that engulfed the city. Elected officials, entertainers (including Anthony Quinn and Fredric March), and trusted newspaper reporters listened attentively. A question arose from the distinguished group: "What can we do to help?" [52]

King stated that they would need lots of money for bail. Belafonte volunteered to organize a fundraising committee, and attendees gave or pledged money for bail bonds. Later, Birmingham county officials adjusted the amount required for protesters to post bond on an appeal in misdemeanor cases from $300 to $2,500. Through Belafonte's influence, the bonds were insured by the Kennedy administration. For three weeks, Belafonte set his formal entertainment engagements aside and helped organize people to solicit funds for the movement.

The Birmingham campaign was the greatest example of King's ability to mobilize a coalition of conscience. After weeks of a successful boycott of white businesses, sit-ins at local restaurants, and nonviolent protests at municipal facilities, local officials decided to contact African-American leaders and open negotiations for a settlement. King did not understate the significance of the Birmingham campaign and its success. He wrote:

> The amazing aftermath of Birmingham, the sweeping Negro Revolution, revealed to people all over the land that there are no outsiders in all these fifty states of America. When a police dog buried his fangs in the ankle of a small child in Birmingham, he buried his fangs in the ankle of every American. The bell of man's inhumanity to man does not toll for any one man. It tolls for you, for me, for all of us.[53]

Newspaper photos and television cameras captured students under attack from police dogs, beaten with police clubs, and sprayed with high-pressure firefighters' water hoses. King's letter became a movement manifesto, which spoke to the heart of issues in the South. The money raised by the athletes and entertainers provided the freedom for King to move in this new direction. The protests and boycotts caused local businesses to lose 98% of African-American customers; over 125 white business leaders were at the mercy of the protesters. At the height of the Birmingham campaign, over 2,500 demonstrators were in jail at one time, and a large percentage of them were youth. [54]

Furthermore, King served as the primary fundraiser for the movement. He faced the dilemma of being in jail and not earning enough money to support the movement or being among the people in the jail cells to show solidarity and his commitment to sacrifice. The civil rights leader looked to others in the north for financial support. Financial support took on a different tone and meaning entirely during the Birmingham campaign. Athletes and entertainers were center stage, and at the center of the stage was Harry Belafonte.

THE MONEY TRAIL

As I continued in my quest to follow the money, I could not believe that I actually got to touch thousands of receipts and hundreds of ledgers for expenses from back then. King and the SCLC often faced financial constraints throughout the civil rights movement. His primary source of income came from speaking honorariums and book royalties. According to the ledgers I examined, the majority of the money allowed King and his team to travel, retain offices, and pay legal expenses.

King learned how to improve the effectiveness of rallies and fundraising from the Reverend Billy Graham's team. All of these types of rallies were typically held in outdoor arenas and took on the aura of political and social pep rallies. They featured a myriad of speakers, including political figures, athletes, and entertainers. The aim of rallies was to drum up support for the movement by using the profile and celebrity status of the affluent and well-connected.

Graham's team explained their strategy of pre-planning for a rally. After carefully choosing a location, they would visit the city three to six months prior to the rally to meet with local pastors, political, and community leaders to discuss the event. They planned everything down to the music, fliers, and the leaders' private luncheon. Everyone connected to the event was asked to fast and pray before the event took place. Prior to meeting with Graham's team, King raised money preaching at local churches, and then gave his honorarium to the SCLC. Graham's advice took him from local churches to thousand seat stadiums. [55]

In 1963, preceding the Birmingham campaign and following the historic March on Washington, no less than twenty-four rallies were held across the nation. As one would expect, big cities like Berkeley ($3,250.00), Milwaukee ($4,002.25), Cleveland ($13,675.69), Philadelphia ($6,750.23), Brooklyn ($3, 9800.43), San Francisco ($11,382.52), and Detroit ($428,732.42) took in the most money for the SCLC. Smaller cities, such as Hartford ($1,267.89), Dover ($2,060.93), Suffolk ($954.00), and Toledo ($1,750.00) gave strong support despite smaller outcomes. [56]

King did not attend all of the rallies. In some instances, members from his staff, including his father – Martin Luther King Sr., his wife - Coretta, or his assistant - Andrew Young spoke in his place. The speaker at the podium was not as important as the reason for which people gathered. This was a testament of King's leadership. He did not need to be at the center of every event in order for people to respond and lend their financial support.

With the help of two key political and celebrity figures, Stanley Levison and Jack O'Dell, King was able to utilize their fundraising expertise. By the end of 1961, they raised over $80,000, which was nearly half of the previous year's budget for the SCLC. At one point, the "Master List" of contributors

soul of America.

King's proposed budgets for concerts included radio and newspaper advertisements, posters, printing a map for distribution of tickets, and seating charts. The estimated cost to host the events was based upon the success of the Belafonte fundraiser. The total proposed budget for the Lena Horne concert was over $11,000, with the net gross projected at $23,777. The budget for Mahalia Jackson's concert was $9,635, with a net gross of $8,160. [60] Constant challenges for King and the SCLC included a lack of organization and adequate systems to maximize the potential of concerts, but the frequency of the concerts allowed King and the SCLC to improve upon their organizational weaknesses.

In June of 1962, Belafonte gave a concert at the Municipal Auditorium in Atlanta. Approximately 4,000 of the 5,000 tickets were sold at prices ranging from $2.50 to $15 each. The event netted the SCLC nearly $24,000.[61] Belafonte later sponsored a series of concerts as part of his European tour; King and his wife accompanied Belafonte, and the movement was the benefactor for proceeds raised.

On December 11, 1962, Sammy Davis, Jr. headlined an event in Westchester County, New York. He danced, sang ballads, and played musical instruments. Davis invited the Hollywood elite. Actor and singer Peter Lawford introduced King, and comedian Pat Henry performed a routine. Over 4,000 people braved the cold to participate in the event. The total cash receipts were $25,638.53. After administrative costs and expenses, SCLC netted $12,750. [62]

None of this could have been possible without King's understanding of money and Belafonte's ability to step up and raise the necessary financial support to make Birmingham and national rallies such a history-making success. That's the power of money.

Even in my own life, it's impossible to separate the opportunities I've had from financial support from others. At times, my family was able to survive because of government support and the benefits from Head Start or lunch programs provided to us by the State of California and federal government. Growing up, money was front and center in the concerns of my mom and all three of us kids. We struggled and there were some difficult days. Mom worked at school and sometimes she brought home leftovers from the cafeteria that became our dinner, like milk that was used for our breakfast. I remember those nights, and every step of the way there was someone who used money to help us move forward in ways we couldn't have without it. Like Deputy Sheriff Rita Hayes, the woman who bought me the first two books I ever owned.

Another woman we called Mother Johnson would take me wherever I wanted to go out to eat when I won track meets in Junior High. At that time, McDonald's was a luxury to our family – we just couldn't afford to go. So every time she would say, "Where do you want to go? My treat!" I would respond: "I want McDonald's!" Eating a Big Mac and getting ice cream on a cone was really a new concept for me so I had to learn how to eat ice cream properly.

Going to college. Owning a home. Attending graduate school. Succeeding at post-graduate school. All of these things in my life were because other people contributed resources to me and my family. Loving money is the root of all kinds of evil, but because people loved me they leveraged their money so that I could give my life in service to others.

I learned from King not to be squeamish about money but to put money in its rightful place – as a tool to be used to serve others. As we lead organizations and families and even ourselves, we have to ask if we're holding back because we're afraid to ask for money or to use money in creative ways to achieve the mission we've been called to do.

So let me ask you:

What is your relationship to what you're doing and to money?

Are there people who are part of your mission who are more capable of raising support for your cause?

If you do have some hesitancy with money, where does it stem from?

Who are the money people in your life?

Who are the people who love to give?

In what ways do you need to grow as a leader to be worthy of stewarding other's money responsibly?

CHAPTER EIGHT

THE POWER OF
RISKS

"There comes a time when one must take a position
that is neither safe, nor politic, nor popular, but he
must take it because conscience tells him it is right."
– Dr. Martin Luther King Jr.

CHAPTER 8

Today, most of the risks we take are geared towards thrill-seeking like skydiving, bungee jumping, and all things considered extreme sports. During the Civil Rights Movement, taking a risk was neither fun nor thrilling. African-Americans who marched or spoke out against the injustices of racial discrimination in the south were beaten or killed as par for the course. Fed up with mistreatment, African-Americans joined King in his efforts to fight against racial injustices.

Although it was a grave risk, the citizens of Alabama were ready for the long haul and boycotted buses in Montgomery for over a year. Nearly 40,000 African-Americans walked to their destinations. After 381 days of boycotts, the Alabama federal courts ruled that segregation was a violation of African-Americans' 14th Amendment right to equal protection. Although a victory, integration led to violence. King, was now thrust in the forefront and risked his life and that of his family during the entire movement. Consider this timeline of events:

January 27, 1956 - Dr. King received a threatening phone call;

January 28, 1956 - Dr. King was arrested and fined for speeding;

January 30, 1956 - In the late evening, Dr. King is speaking at a mass meeting at the Montgomery Improvement Association to encourage its members to continue the bus boycott;

January 30, 1956 - At 9:15 PM, King's home is bombed with his wife and daughter inside. Fortunately they are not injured. [63]

When King found out about the bombing of his home, he rushed home and stood outside and addressed a group of angry citizens who wanted to retaliate. King urged the crowd to remain calm as violence was not the answer. What would you have done?

"GO FROM YOUR COUNTRY, YOUR PEOPLE AND YOUR FATHER'S HOUSEHOLD

TO THE LAND I WILL SHOW YOU."

GENESIS 12:1

JAMES BYUN Ph.D.

PASTOR

LIFESPRING CHURCH, SEOUL, KOREA.

LIFESPRINGKOREA.ORG

James served as an international consultant for Fortune 500 companies while serving in local communities of faith in San Francisco, California, and Dallas, Texas. With no supporting missions organization or start-up members, but in simple obedience to God's call, he packed up his family, including his four young children, and left the comforts of familiar surroundings and moved to plant a church in the Songdo area of Incheon, South Korea. Although he is Korean by heritage, he grew up in America and barely spoke any Korean. I had the pleasure of traveling to Korea to speak to our US troops, and while there visited James and his family. I dedicated and offered a prayer in what would become their main sanctuary. Starting with just three members, in less than four years, Lifespring Church has grown exponentially in size and influence. The church represents 32 nations and has sister churches in both South Korea and San Francisco, California. James utilizes his consulting skills to help revitalize local communities of faith. James' passion remains palpable, and like King, James wasn't afraid to ask and take a risk and heed God's call.

Taking risks involves doing something out of the ordinary with an expectation of a unique life-changing event. However, it is more than an expectation, it is a deeply held belief that one is going to achieve his or her goal. Risk-takers are confident in their actions and, like King, know the importance of buy-in from the mainstream celebrities like athletes and entertainers. Every athlete and entertainer who aligned with King was a risk-taker. Jackie Robinson not only broke the color barrier in Major League Baseball, endured taunts on and off the field, and withstood death threats, but his decision to side with King exposed him and his family to more danger.

Robinson is celebrated today—not only for his accomplishments on the field, but also for his willingness to risk and engage in social activism off the field. He confronted U.S. presidents, marched with the underprivileged, and offered his name to the Civil Rights Movement.

During the 1960s, the United States Government saw the Civil Rights Movement as a threat. Phones were tapped. People were followed. Monies were traced and tracked. So in order for those involved with Civil Rights to protect their freedom of privacy as well as increase their chances of success, they had to move money around outside the bank system, much like the mob in Las Vegas or the Mafia in Chicago.

One such time, King asked Harry Belafonte if he would transport $70,000 (or a little over half a million dollars in today's money) from Los Angeles to Mississippi. Belafonte accepted the mission and invited Sidney Poitier to travel south and make good on a promise to deliver money to the SCLC. Belafonte and Poitier traveled to a small airstrip and the two caught a prop plane and flew to Mississippi.

What they hoped to be a simple flight and transfer of money turned into a life-or-death confrontation with the Klu Klux Klan. When they landed in Mississippi, they were being followed and eventually chased by what they believed to be the KKK while driving on a dark road. Eventually they lost the pursuers, but still had to deliver the money as well as attend a rally for voter registration. Against their better judgment, they remained overnight and spoke at the rally, but they spent their night under security. When they finally returned to Los Angeles, Sidney turned to Harry and said with a sigh (and in far more colorful language than I use here as the author): "Don't ever ask me to do something like that again."

On June 12, 1963, actors Paul Newman and Marlon Brando joined the Congress on Racial Equality on the steps of Sacramento to advocate for passage of a fair-housing bill.[64]

In early August, 1963, the two joined forces again by traveling to Alabama. African-Americans were protesting unfair and unequal hiring practices of local and state agencies in Gadsden, Alabama. Governor George Wallace, who represented the status quo of bigotry and racism, stood aside and watched as Brando and Newman boarded a bus en route to a Birmingham rally. The state's top executive did not welcome the entertainers.[65]

On January 16, 1965, the American Football League scheduled its annual all-star game at New Orleans's Tulane Stadium. Twenty-one African-American players protested the game's location, based upon the city's overt policies of discrimination. Cabdrivers, hotels, and local restaurants were on record in refusing their requests for services. The discriminatory practices were in conflict with the 1964 Civil Rights Act. African-Americans accounted for 40% of the teams, thus making them a valuable commodity. The league resisted and made proverbial threats if players followed through on plans of a formal walk-out.[66]

African-American players were joined by white players and presented a united front of protests. Both groups of players made good on their promise to boycott. The venue was changed by Commissioner Joe Foss to Houston, Texas. The AFL players' actions came despite risks of suspension and loss of financial compensation. King did not formally organize the boycott, but as Maureen Smith described, it was the first example of a professional sport in which a group of athletes was able to use the nonviolent direct action methods used by King. The players noted King's demonstrated acts of sacrifice and challenge as part of their motivation for collective action.[67]

Comedian Dick Gregory was not shy in taking risks; the FBI investigated the Chicago native for his involvement in the Civil Rights Movement. Gregory was an outspoken critic of the federal government (Kennedy and Johnson administrations), as well as local municipal governments. He attended rallies, marches, voter registration meetings, proposed strategies for protests, and conducted benefit concerts. When Civil Rights Leader James Meredith was ambushed on a highway in Mississippi, Gregory was the first to arrive at the hospital to express his comfort to the victim. He pledged to move forward with Meredith's "march against fear." Upon the disappearance of three voter registration workers in Mississippi, Gregory called on the Kennedy administration officials to devote all the necessary resources to finding them.[68]

Greenwood, Mississippi, was one of the region's top producers of cotton. In 1962, droughts and famine hit farmers. But the greatest threats were not to their crops but to their physical and emotional well being as fear escalated among African-Americans in their attempts to become registered voters. Gregory was the first celebrity to set up camp and stand side-by-side with local farmers. He donated tons of food to offset their loss of income and lend support to struggling families. Historian and scholar Taylor Branch noted that Gregory was moved by the stories of struggle and poverty. Later, Gregory stood alongside James Baldwin in Selma, a city the poet described as one of the worst places he had ever visited with respect to police brutality and anger from local whites. At risk to his life, Gregory escorted citizens to the steps of the county courthouses to register.[69]

In 1966, Gregory joined King in Chicago to protest the dilapidated housing conditions in Chicago's ghettos. Riots and violence broke out from a sea of frustration. Gregory echoed King, calling for young African-Americans not to take to the streets, inflict violence, or destroy public and private property. His bold confrontation with political officials in comedic forums gave him tremendous credibility among average citizens and civil rights leaders. He was viewed as a person who was committed to do whatever was necessary to advance the Civil Rights Movement. Average protesters who witnessed his blatant disregard for whites in authority lived vicariously through his rebellion. The impact of Gregory's words fortified the resolve of African-Americans to demand a future where equality was not the exception, but the moral rule that governed the nation. Gregory was asked by reporters whether he feared for his career or loss of economic earnings as a result of his outspokenness on civil rights. Gregory replied:

> No. It's a funny thing. People who would never get out on the front lines come to a club where I'm playing. It's their way of showing support. A few years back, when I was just making jokes, and was not as active in the movement as I am now, people would write me letters and call me "nigger." Now, I still get letters of protest and hostility, but they say "Mr. Gregory."[70]

Actress, singer, and dancer Josephine Baker suffered financial loss and hardship because of her outspokenness against America's treatment of its citizens. She adopted nearly twenty orphans from various nationalities and experiences. The intent of this was to convince the world that the greatest method to overcoming racism was love. The innocence of children exemplified her belief. Despite personal and professional risks, she maintained her commitment to King and the movement he led. Baker sent money and notes of encouragement to King, despite her fragile success and constant challenge of scrutiny and persecution by the Kennedy and Johnson administrations.

Baker was the target of FBI investigations dating back as far as the 1950s. As they did with Dick Gregory, the State Department made efforts to mute her protest against the United States. Baker was the focus of government investigations for Communist affiliations during the Civil Rights Movement. The government's scrutiny of Baker intensified as her allegiance to King and her involvement in the movement became more visible. As she was attempting to return to the US from France for a benefit concert with King, in December 1963, the State Department denied her reentry. She risked her international stage prominence to draw attention to racial injustice within the United States. The State Department informed neighboring nations of her alleged association with Communist countries (namely Peru, Columbia, Cuba, and Haiti).[71]

In concert with other organizations and individuals of goodwill, athletes and entertainers must be willing to use their positions of influence with people and power struggles afforded to them by virtue of their celebrity status. Harry Belafonte, Sidney Poitier, Dick Gregory and Josephine Baker were among those who made sacrifices because of King's leadership. Civil rights legislation and the Martin Luther King, Jr. National Holiday are examples of what can happen when such partnerships occur.

ON THE FRONT LINES

One of the highlights of my life happened on my 40th birthday. I was fortunate to travel on a whirlwind trip to South Korea. I left Los Angeles on April 6th to fly to Seoul and return within seventy-two hours. I was invited to conduct a training and leadership development session for the Airborne Military Division of the United States Army. I have always had respect for our women and men in the U.S. armed forces. In fact, whenever I am with my family and we see people in uniform, we go out of our way to greet them and thank them for their service. A small gesture, but it represents my enormous gratitude for their bravery and sacrifice.

When I arrived at Incheon International Airport, I was greeted by a Sergeant First Class. He held a white sign with my name so I waved and headed towards him with a warm smile.

"Welcome to Seoul, Dr. Goodloe." He shook my hand firmly.

"Thank you, Sergeant."

We headed down a busy corridor to a car directly outside the airport entrance. As we drove, we made small talk about my flight and the Lakers' losing season.

Just before I arrived on the military base in Seoul, I was required to watch a training video and sign off on paperwork regarding my visit. The video began with the US Army General stating, "In the event of an attack by the North Koreans, our first priority is to defend our allies here and to protect our US personnel and interest...that includes you!" I thought to myself, this is not a normal leadership development conference training I am conducting. In all honesty, I was a bit nervous. I had some concern for my safety and well- being. Initially, I felt out of my comfort zone. I was exhausted from my flight and ten plus hours of watching my favorite action show, 24, by way of DVD. Everything about this trip seemed larger than life; the soldiers I met, the base I was housed in, and the moment I was about to step into. Despite the bravery I watched on the screen which was acted out by Kiefer Sutherland, the star of the 24, I had not gained any of his confidence.

Part of the reason for my discomfort was that before I arrived, the North Koreans conducted unprovoked hostile military action towards the South Koreans, and tensions were high. Several artillery shells were fired onto the South Korean island of Yeonpyeong, about two miles from the

Northern Limit Line (the disputed sea between North and South Korea). Nearly all of the island's 1,600 residents fled for cover, while two South Korean soldiers were killed and nearly a dozen were injured. It was one of the most intense and deliberate acts of provocation in recent months, and I was headed there.

Within a few short days, it became clear to me what it means to be on the front lines. I saw women and men on their military assignment post, armed, ready, and willing to confront any potential threat. I remember how young they looked, while at the same time thinking that what they were prepared to do, if necessary, required the highest levels of maturity and bravery. Those few days in Korea made me even more proud of the job being done by our military. They are risking their lives to protect us, and they do so daily with the utmost resolve, commitment, and professionalism.

To date, we have roughly 30,000 U.S. troops in the region and a joint partnership with our allies from South Korea. I was fascinated by the discipline, focus, commitment, and leadership by both military forces. The attention to detail was beyond anything I had seen within an organization or any group of people. From the logistics of getting me there and providing everything I needed, to making sure I had the necessary information about the challenges they wanted me to address, the United States Army was first class. I wanted for nothing. I met squadron leaders from the Blackhawk and Apache helicopter divisions, along with members of their support team.

I was invited to take a simulated flight in one of the airships, and it was unlike any experience I had ever known. Every video game I had played and every amusement park ride I had experienced, from my childhood throughout my adulthood, paled in comparison to what I felt inside that simulator. The Apache helicopter and other aircraft in its division, including the Black Hawk, were nicknamed Death Dealers by the soldiers. The name says it all. What these machines can do with skilled pilots guiding their every move is frightening to say the least, yet pretty awesome.

When I look at the historical record of athletes and entertainers who worked with King, I think of women and men on the front lines. Their careers, families, and lives were in danger, yet they made their voices known by offering their talents, gifts, and resources to a cause greater than themselves. The Civil Rights Movement was a time in our nation's history when many witnessed and experienced the worst of our nation's demons. Hatred, racism, discrimination, and injustice were the norm. Yet, it was also a time when we witnessed ordinary women and men become instruments of change for a society that desperately needed to chart a different course: one towards justice, equality, peace, and liberty for all. Athletes and entertainers were on the front lines and were led by the greatest leader of the latter half of the twentieth century: Reverend Dr. Martin Luther King Jr.

What cause would you risk your life for?

What wrongs are the norms in your context, and what are you willing to do about them?

What fears do you have that preclude you from moving forward with others in risking some...to gain much more?

Closer to Home

The year was 1996. Churches were being burned. Fear was in the air. Local, state, and federal authorities had little evidence to go on to show who was responsible for the rash of arson violence taking place in Boligee, Alabama. Local chapters of the NAACP and SCLC, as well as faith organizations issued a clarion call to the nation to help them rebuild their houses of worship and to stand with them on matters of justice and peace. I experienced a small dose of what African-Americans experienced in 1956. At the time, I was in my third year of seminary living in San Francisco and serving as the Youth Pastor at the historic Allen Temple Baptist Church, in Oakland, California. Our church joined other local congregations in taking up offering collections to give to those adversely impacted by the burnings. As money began to pour in, I was asked by my pastor, Dr. J. Alfred Smith, Sr., to co-lead a delegation of goodwill efforts with another bay area church, Lafayette Orinda Presbyterian Church. We opened a special fund with a branch of Wells Fargo Bank, took out ads in local papers, and placed announcements in our church bulletins. We collected money from our respective communities of faith, other organizations, and the public to support those who were adversely impacted by violent acts of hatred and destruction of property.

The decision was made to not only send money, but

to send a team that would go and help in the rebuilding efforts in Boligee. I was reluctant. I felt inadequate, and, for a moment, even fearful. I had no practical skill set to offer. I was young. People were committing acts of violence against the very people I was asked to come help. Something stirred inside me and I knew I had to go. I had a willing heart. For several years, I was trained and discipled by one of the leading pioneers in activism and justice Christendom had known: J. Alfred Smith, Sr. A big part of his teaching and activism was taking risk for justice and peace, and for the least and left out. I was a student and activism became my way of life. I had to go. Taking risks for what I strongly believed was the right thing to do, was the only option.

Within a two-month period of time, we went to the South and raised over $75,000. We recruited people from our communities who were skilled in areas that would be of great importance once we were on the ground: carpenters, electricians, brick masons, engineers, and lighting technicians were among the people who were part of our team. Several dozen of us boarded planes headed to Alabama. Quakers, Methodists, Baptists, Pentecostals, and Jews were all part of the collective effort to make a difference. There were some people who did not come from a particular faith background, but read the reports of what we were preparing to do and were eager and committed to join our journey. That day, we were part of a "coalition of conscience," one of risks, goodwill, and faith.

Before we arrived from the Bay Area, we heard

rumors about pending threats that awaited us in Boligee, yet we were determined to let our voices be heard, put our money to good use, and use our hammers and plywood saws to create beauty from destruction. As a young seminarian, it was the most impactful time of my education and ministry career. No lecture I ever heard and no book I ever read changed my life more than the pilgrimage to Boligee, Alabama. It was a defining moment in my life, my church, and for those we partnered with from other faith communities in the Bay Area, and most certainly for the people of Boligee. I was in the company of risk-takers.

I stood in places where choir stands and pulpits were positioned, only to be replaced by charred beams and concrete structures that gave way to immeasurable heat caused by fire. I can't remember a night or morning that I did not cry. For more than a week, we built churches in the sweltering heat, which only the South could offer. In the early mornings, we prayed together and sang songs to lift the spirits of the local parishioners and pastors. By night, we held worship services and were strengthened by listening to stories of challenge and triumph, both from the scriptures as well as the local residents who worked alongside us daily in the rebuilding efforts. To be honest, we were encouraged by them more than they were by us at times. We were all deeply impacted by their resolve and emboldened by their courage and refusal to match hate for hate to those responsible for destroying their houses of worship. How could people be filled with such hate in the time and period we were living in? I thought. After all, we were decades removed from the era of civil rights.

When I arrived back to our church, I was asked by members to share my experiences with our community as well as the staff and leaders who supported our efforts. I spoke to members of a local Jewish Temple to share a special evening of commemoration and celebrations for those who journeyed with us from their house of worship. I shared words on behalf of my church; this was a great honor, and something I would have never experienced had I not taken the risk to travel to Boligee in the first place. I remember being extremely nervous, more so than usual for some reason. It was my first time speaking in a Jewish temple, but not my first time speaking in front of large audiences. I gave thought and reflections on my time spent with women and men who were part of the delegation who traveled with me to the South. As I stood to speak, I felt at peace and the words offered were not my own but were taken from the Old Testament prophet Micah, Chapter Six: the people of Israel were not honoring God with their words, hearts, and actions. A rhetorical question was put forth as to what God required of them to make things right in their relationship with the Transcendent and with each other. The prophet responded:

"He has shown you, O mortal, what is good. And what does the Lord require of you? To act justly and to love mercy and to walk humbly with your God."[72]

I cried as I shared that Friday night. But my tears were of joy and deep affection for what I had witnessed with my own eyes and experienced from the depths of my being during that life-changing journey. The capacity of the human spirit to show kindness, love mercy, and walk humbly with God was more real than ever before. In the face of brokenness, we helped to create beauty. In the midst of burned out buildings, we were blessed beyond measure. We were determined to counterbalance acts of selfishness with acts of selflessness and to confront acts of hate with acts of love. We all shared a common bond of taking risks to serve the needs of others. Martin Luther King, Jr. made this observation years ago in speaking on the matter of taking risks and in matching acts of darkness with acts of light:

> "When evil men plot, good men must plan. When evil men burn and bomb, good men must build and bind. When evil men shout words of hatred, good men must commit themselves to the glories of love. Where evil men would seek to perpetuate an unjust status quo, good men must seek to bring into being a real order of justice."[73]

CHAPTER NINE

THE POWER OF
CREATIVITY

MAKE IT BETTER

"We must use time creatively--and forever realize that time is always hope to do great things."

– Dr. Martin Luther King Jr.

CHAPTER 9

Creativity is the ability to make new things or think of new ideas. Leaders must have the ability to be creative: not so much in an artistic way, but in the ability to change perspective in real time when the original strategy isn't working. Being creative involves a bit of risk-taking when so-called experts advise of a course of action, and as a leader, you choose what's in your heart. Great leaders know when to lean into the new and when to improve upon the good. History shows us that great doesn't happen by accident. When it comes to the great speeches of the 20th Century, Martin Luther King Jr.'s speech originally called, "I Have a Dream" is undoubtedly included on any list. Most of us have heard it several times and we see familiar grainy footage of King with his hand raised in front of 250,000 people on the steps of the Lincoln Memorial on a humid August in 1963.

The 1963 March on Washington was the largest organized protest in the nation's history at the time. The march was the second most significant historical event in King's leadership with athletes and entertainers, who played a key role in the proceedings leading up to the march and its execution—more so than the Birmingham campaign. The volume of participants and the logistics involved in putting the march together are reasons for it to be considered the apex of the Civil Rights Movement. The march brought visibility across the nation, as the Civil Rights Movement brought scores of groups and individuals together across demographic, ethnic, and social lines and propelled the movement for coming challenges.

BEHIND THE DREAM

On July 2, 1963, King flew to New York at the request of A. Phillip Randolph to meet with four other civil rights leaders: Roy Wilkins of the NAACP, John Lewis of SNCC, James Farmer of the Congress of Racial Equality, and Whitney Young of the Urban League. The goal was to put the final logistics and touches to the March on Washington, including garnering publicity, preparing food for marchers, establishing restroom facilities, ordering the day's program, soliciting media coverage, and organizing transportation to and from the march for participants.

King charged Belafonte with gathering the support of entertainers. On July 23, 1963, King sent a telegram to Belafonte. King wrote on behalf of the committee members:

> We feel that the effectiveness of the march can be tremendously aided by the presence and participation of a large number of theatrical and artistic personalities of our nation. The presence of such popular idols and well-known national and international figures will have a tremendous impact on the congressmen (sic) and senators whose votes will be needed to get the bill through. Therefore I proposed to the committee that we seek to develop a Celebrity Plane from CA to NY. I can think of none who can best implement this idea than you. [74]

Belafonte accepted King's challenge.

Several weeks before the March on Washington, the public was not aware that there were athletes and entertainers behind the scenes meeting with congressmen and congresswomen. They didn't know that Marlon Brando, Harry Belafonte, Lena Horne, Joan Baez, Charleton Heston, Paul Newman, Sammy Davis, Jr. and others had their assignments to not only attend the march, but to knock on the doors of congress, introduce themselves, and to lobby on behalf of the Civil Rights Movement legislation that was before Congress for a vote.

On the day of the March, Belafonte chartered a plane and organized the attendees, which included Charlton Heston, Peter Lawford, and Joan Baez (who sang the first song over the public address system). Brando twirled a cattle prod in his hands to symbolize acts of police brutality, while Jackie Robinson abandoned the celebrity section in order to sit with people void of notoriety. Others on hand included James Garner, Dick Gregory, Diahann Carroll, and Josephine Baker. Peter, Paul, and Mary rendered a stirring version of Bob Dylan's "Blowin' in the Wind," and—to the crowd's surprise– Dylan joined them onstage in a tribute to Medgar Evers. [75]

Throughout the day there was chaos backstage as leaders of the Movement fought for the vision of what that day was meant to be and who would be included and excluded. James Baldwin was not on the list to speak, and he made his disappointment known to King and others for his exclusion.

There were 15 people in line to speak or perform on

stage before King finally made his way to the podium. After a brief introduction from A. Phillip Randolph, who was titled the "Dean of The Negro Leaders," [76] King took the stage to address an increasingly weary crowd. Not many people are aware of the fact that the most memorable speech of the 20th century almost didn't happen. As King took the stage on that day he held in his hands sheets of paper with his remarks typed up, with notes scribbled in the margins and on the back along with hand-written modifications and lines crossed out. Amidst all the additions and subtractions, nowhere was the phrase "I have a dream" found in the text.

By all accounts King hadn't included the I have a dream wording in his speech. He, his speechwriter, Clarence Jones, a lawyer and senior advisor, Wyatt Walker, and Stanley Levison, had worked tirelessly on crafting a speech more in line with the tone of Abraham Lincoln's Gettysburg Address, since the speech was in the shadow of his legacy, both literally as well as symbolically. In fact, Walker specifically told King not to use the "I Have a Dream" speech, citing that it was "clichéd" and – most surprisingly – that "he had used it too many times already." In fact, King had given the speech a few months earlier in Chicago and had used the refrain again at a rally in Detroit two months earlier. Recently, a restored audio of King's "I Have a Dream" speech was discovered during an address in 1962 at Booker T. Washington High School in Rocky Mount, North Carolina. [77]

King started in with his prepared remarks. Activist, and now Georgia Congressman, John Lewis, who was there that day and had spoken earlier, later recalled that he "thought it was a good speech, but not nearly as powerful as others I'd heard him make." [78] It seemed as though King could also sense that the speech wasn't going as well as he had hoped.

The world-acclaimed musician, Mahalia Jackson, who had sung just hours before him – a woman to whom King had become close through their work together in the Civil Rights Movement – cried out with words of encouragement that changed the face of history forever.

"Tell 'em about the dream, Martin!"

As King was concluding his speech, "Go back to the slums and ghettos of our northern cities, knowing that somehow this situation can and will be changed..." [79]

Mahalia called out again, "Tell 'em about the dream, Martin!"

At that moment, King shifted his weight, set his prepared remarks down on the podium, and uttered these words, "So even though we face the difficulties of today and tomorrow...I still have a dream." [80]

King's speechwriter, Jones, leaned over to a friend and said, "Those people don't know it, but they're about to go to church." [81] Years later, as a young man, I remember watching a well-respected preacher of the 20th century named E.V. Hill who preached an entire sermon on the subject "Say it Again!" His thesis was that there was power in what had been preached before and so why not say it again? King, for all intent and purposes, said it again!

BETTER THAN BEFORE

King used that small moment in time to take something that was good and make it great. According to King, the coalition of conscience was at its best during the March on Washington. Speaking to the importance and magnitude of King's speech, the march, and the vision he offered as a leader that day, Danah Zohar and Ian Marshall wrote:

> Dr. King's words reached beyond the given realities of American race relations and painted the picture of a new, more just and loving society scarcely imagined by the American people at that time. He palpably ached in the whole of his being for the not-yet-born, and that ache carried in his voice as an inspirational longing. This... is a vital feature of great visions. They reach deep into the well of human potentiality and present us with the not-yet born. They make us dream...They make us long. They motivate us. [82]

ART
IMITATES
LIFE

JAMES WILLIAMS

FOUNDER

RAKING LEAVES PRODUCTION

DEEPWILLIAMS.COM

James Williams is one of the most powerful men I know. His physical presence and stature is a given. But what makes James most intriguing is his compassion, gentleness, and creativity. James has dedicated his life to serving others as a father, husband, and as a business professional to some of the most influential people in the entertainment industry. James is also a filmmaker. Raking Leaves Production (RLP) is his gift to the world. An independent film company committed to creating and telling stories on matters of justice and social welfare including adoption and foster care, as well as race relations, and equality is the heartbeat of RLP. My family and I have had the privilege along with others to support James and his dreams along the way as a filmmaker. James' film Palms (a film based upon adoption) won the 2013 International Family Film Festival, Hollywood, California. Most importantly, humanity wins by the advocacy James gives to causes through the medium of film. Mr. James Williams is a King Maker!

King's speech gave America an opportunity to have its finest moment and usher in a new era in human relations, [83] all because he took something that was good and made it better. Since there was no time for King to create something new, his instinct allowed him to make something old better. There is real power in taking something that's working, something that has potential, and making it even better. There's power in taking a good relationship and making it great. There's power in taking your leadership that's good and making it great, even when the temptation is to jump into something else, to engage in the addictive thrill of starting over, of doing something people have never heard before or seen before.

I remember when I moved from a predominantly African-American church in Dallas, Texas to be part of Mosaic – a young and diverse faith community in Los Angeles. The culture change was huge. The way Mosaic talked about the scriptures and life and creativity was vastly different from how I had been trained as an orator. As an art form, communication looked vastly different from what I had been taught. I was eager to learn and spent years intentionally growing so that I could communicate in the most persuasive, authentic, and powerful way possible in whatever context I found myself in. Years after moving, I can proudly say having been in that context has made a profoundly positive impact on my communication skills, and I'm forever grateful for being given the opportunity to serve in such a different environment. That process wasn't easy. I had a lot to learn. It would have been far easier to just say, "I got this whole communication thing down." But I wanted to learn; I wanted to grow. I wanted to be faithful to the skillset God had given me. I wanted to push the boundaries of what I was good at to see if I could be truly great at something. I wanted to take an encouraging message and present it beautifully.

In my own life, one of my commitments as a speaker is to never give the exact talk twice. It is challenging to take ancient truths and make them fresh and relevant for today. However, I never feel like I've mastered it. When I'm communicating what I believe is the most important message in the world, I still get this feeling that it can never be good enough. The truth is, I've devoted most of my life to improving as a speaker. Staying up to date on current events, spending time with different people of all cultures and ethnicities, and learning to listen to their souls' longings so that I can communicate more effectively with them remains a constant in my life. These are lifelong pursuits that have shaped my life.

Think about the things you do well. Think about the things you do that are almost great, that – with a little more intentionality – with a little more polish – with a little more TLC, could be something really special. Think about the things in your life that have potential. Not a little bit of potential, but a lot of potential. Think about the people in your organization who are really good, but not yet great. Think about the projects or skills or opportunities that you know with a little bit of added energy could create exponential results.

Think about your best moments – your moments of high performance – your best presentations, your best meetings, your best ideas. Is there any life left in them?

What if your most powerful gifts and opportunities were right under your nose and you didn't even realize it? What if you already had your I- Have-a-Dream moment, but just not in the context you are currently in? I know it sounds like blasphemy. It may sound like microwaved leftovers. Let me be clear: I love creativity, and I hate tradition for tradition's sake. But every now and then the old things or words make for the best great moment.

Ultimately that's what making it better is all about. It's about saying something well, not necessarily new. It's about saying something again and again and again. Not because it needs to be new, but because it needs to be said. When we do, we begin to step into our greatness in ways we never dreamed possible. King wasn't going to tell people about his dream. Yet because of Mahalia Jackson's encouragement, he not only reiterated a previous message, but he did so in a new context. In sharing his dream it was creative and helped make that dream come true for many others then and today.

What have you done that is good?

How can you make it better?

• • •

I'll be honest, I love new. It reminds me of progress. I like new because it reminds me of originality. The smell of new. The texture of new. The promise that it has for the not yet having been explored. I also enjoy new because of the bragging rights like when you show up with the newest gadget or have seen the latest movie. Maybe I should be ashamed to admit it, but I've been guilty of rubbing the new in others' faces more than once.

We stand in line for hours to buy it, we find ourselves

constantly updating our apps and wardrobes. Our news programs have violated every principle of journalism ever created so that we can have breaking news. Our news anchors tell us that it's too early to speculate, followed by an hour of speculation. We have conferences to unveil the new. Apple. Amazon. GM. It's exciting. It's intoxicating. We spend as much money introducing the new as we do creating something new. Recently, I watched a live interview of a former congresswoman who specialized in national security being conducted in light of unsettling events in the Middle East. In mid-sentence the award-winning, veteran news anchor, with over thirty years of experience, interrupted the interview to go to breaking live images of a young teen pop star being released from a local county jail after speeding and disorderly conduct charges were filed. The interview eventually continued, after an apology from the anchor, but ironically the crisis still continues in that region of the world, and I believe the charges for the teen heart-throb were dropped.

We love the new, and sometimes we trick ourselves into believing that new is always better. In fact, we live in an age that is addicted to the new or what economist Nassim Taleb calls "neophilila." New phone, new TV, new car, new clothes, new toys, even new relationships. When something gets a little old, we're taught that it's time to replace it with something new.

Now obviously there's nothing wrong with new, but my point is that there's nothing inherently good about it either. Some people don't like the new because they're traditionalists. They're clinging to the past. They're afraid of change and they see new as the enemy of the status quo. The reality is that new is the enemy of the status quo. And that's a good thing. But new is sometimes also the enemy of something else – something we may not always realize. I'm convinced that the greatest challenge with the new is not that it's the enemy of the average, but that it's the nemesis of great.

Sometimes we get so stuck in pursuing the new that we rarely become great. Imagine if athletes wanted to change sports every year: "Have you heard about this new sport? It's all the rage." They may have a great experience, but they'd never know how it feels to be great at one sport. Or imagine never picking a major in school and just taking random classes. One might learn a lot, but she would never graduate. That person might know a little about everything, but never know enough about something to get a decent job.

CHAPTER TEN

THE POWER TO
DREAM

What happens to a dream deferred?
Does it dry up
like a raisin in the sun?
Or fester like a sore--
And then run?
Does it stink like rotten meat?
Or crust and sugar over--
like a syrupy sweet?
Maybe it just sags
like a heavy load.

Or does it explode?

– Langston Hughes

CHAPTER TEN

A Final Word To Athletes, Entertainers and Others of Public Influence

King had the ability to relate to athletes and entertainers. He spoke with moral clarity and called them to higher levels of understanding and social responsibility. This brought a new meaning to the word "greatness" in the eyes of athletes and entertainers. As part of its *Content of Character* series, ESPN Sports held a town-hall meeting at the historic Ebenezer Baptist Church in Atlanta, Georgia, to discuss the state of progress for African-American athletes since King's death.

In the two-hour, nationally televised event, the panelists included noteworthy sports and entertainment figures like acclaimed film director Spike Lee, NCAA Basketball Coach John Calipari, critically acclaimed sports journalist Michael Wilbon, and former University of Miami Coach Randy Shannon. [84] The topics discussed covered minority representation in top positions of professional and collegiate sports, media scrutiny, coverage of athletes who had made poor moral choices, and the idea of athletes maximizing their buying power and images.

The speakers failed to mention King's call for athletes and entertainers to leverage their influence and bring constructive change to the social and moral conditions of his day. Issues of shared sacrifice on the part of athletes and entertainers and the risk to their careers and lives failed to receive a voice in the special. Yet, this was a major part of King's legacy.

Bob Ley, one of two co-hosts for the town-hall meeting, raised the question of social responsibility by name, but the panelists turned the conversation toward issues surrounding athletes' personal gains and interests. An examination of King's leadership with athletes and entertainers reveals their capacity to do and become more, when they respond to the call.

King certainly promoted and advocated for personal gain for athletes and entertainers, as well as for all Americans, but that never came at the expense of the wider social responsibility to redeem the soul of America. King was not an athlete, but he understood the political and symbolic importance of sports. The town-hall meeting speakers failed to mention King's leadership with baseball great Jackie Robinson or Muhammad Ali, who joined the Civil Rights Movement to improve the moral health of the nation, not simply to further their own careers. No discussion ensued of Ali's courageous stance and sacrifice to protest the nation's war practices and policies in Vietnam, and the role that King played as a counselor to Ali. At the threat of imprisonment and the loss of economic and social stability, Ali chose to be a fighter outside the boxing ring by becoming a conscientious objector of the Vietnam War; King was literally by his side.

The town-hall series is one glaring example of the gap that exists between the realities of King's leadership with athletes and entertainers forty years ago and what is known by leaders, as well as athletes and entertainers, today. Based upon the nature of the discussions, the leaders on the panel were unaware of the deeper levels of social responsibility to which King issued a clarion call for athletes and entertainers to play a significant role in redeeming the soul of America that still echoes today.

I'm convinced that there has never been a better time for our nation's athletes and entertainers to reclaim the tradition modeled for them by King and the Civil Rights Movement. In the wake of events in Ferguson, Baltimore, Miami, New Orleans, New York City, North Carolina, Los Angeles, and countless other racial and social injustices happening every day around our country, now is the time for athletes and entertainers to steward their influence and create the most positive change. Just imagine how much more progress could be made towards racial equality if there was one athlete, entertainer, or person of influence willing to carry the torch and be a Kingmaker? Just one in each of the 50 states. What if there were two? This was Dr. King's dream and it has undoubtedly become mine. The dream has been deferred far too long.

THE
GLORY
OF
LEARNING

JOHN LEGEND
FOUNDER
SHOW ME CAMPAIGN

SHOWMECAMPAIGN.ORG

John Legend is a household name as a singer, songwriter, and actor. He has won nine Grammy Awards, a Golden Globe, and an Academy Award. As an advocate for social justice and change, John has been actively involved in improving the lives of youth for several years. In 2007, he founded the Show Me Campaign to break the cycles of poverty to offer every child access to quality education. At the age of 15, he won an essay competition in which he described his dream of becoming a recording artist to use his fame and resources to change communities by standing for social justice and equality. John credits the work of Dr. Martin Luther King Jr. in his call to action. He is passionate about the school-to-prison mass incarceration system that disproportionately represents the poor and minorities. Systematic problems in the U.S. criminal justice system led John to embark upon a five-year campaign, Free America, which aims to end mass incarceration. In John's words, "We know right now, that the struggle for freedom and justice is real." John's dream of being a King Maker is alive and well. Glory!

KING MAKER: GOOD STEWARDS

Athletes and entertainers possess incomprehensible financial resources and exposure. They are among the leading income earners and often represent their sporting arenas, artistic mediums, city, or state to a global audience. Los Angeles Lakers basketball player Kobe Bryant's jersey is among the top selling jerseys in the NBA (including the United States and Europe). When the Lakers travel, they hold the title of being the number one desired team to watch, away from their home court. This is in large part because of one man: #24.

After his initial reprieve from professional basketball, Michael Jordan still ranks number one as the most admired athletes in the world. Sports researcher Kenneth Cortsen argues that Jordan's impact can be seen in everything from fragrances, movies, as well as books, shoes, clothing, and video games. The result is undeniable, Cortsen concludes. In short, Jordan is not only the most successful professional basketball player of his time (6 NBA Championships, 6-Time NBA Finals MVP, 5-Time Regular Season MVP, 10th All Time Leading Scorer, Rookie of the Year, 2-Time Olympic Gold Medal winner, and 14 All-Star selections), he is undoubtedly the most transcendent sports figure "brand" of his era.

Country/pop music star Taylor Swift is in a league of her own when it comes to influence. Her 2014 album, *1989*, became the second biggest selling album of that year in one week. In addition, it was the only album to go double platinum at that time. Swift has millions of fans on social media. In 2015, Swift protested Apple's policy of free music downloads by artists in a series of tweets. She argued that the policy was wrong and precluded artists from earning appropriate royalties based upon their work. Within hours a reply was given that the policy would be changed, as Eddy Cue, Apple's Vice President of Internet Software and Services, responded via Twitter back to the celebrated artist, "We hear you @2taylorswift13."[85] Artists like Swift, and athletes like Jordan and Bryant have platforms that reach beyond what they do on stage or on the basketball court. Simply put, people hear them.

Tiger Woods is said to be the world's first billion-dollar athlete. Week after week, television ratings and economic markets are influenced by Woods' presence on the golf course. At Woods' debut in 1996, nine players on the Professional Golf Association (PGA) circuit made one million or more. That same year, Woods announced he was becoming a professional and signed a forty-million-dollar deal with Nike. By 2009, ninety-one players made a million dollars or more on the PGA tour. From prize money, product endorsements, television contracts, and corporate sponsorships, Woods has single-handedly caused a seismic shift in the economy of the nation, not simply the PGA.

Today there are significant causes that can benefit from Bryant, Jordan, and Woods offering their collective voices of support: racial tensions, equal opportunities in executive levels of sports, and human rights. At a minimum, the issues these individuals agree to adopt would gain broad attention worldwide. Businesses, Wall Street, political leaders, civil rights organizations, professional sports leagues, and entertainment studies would take notice. Others from similar professions and points of influences would consider their roles in society.

One way athletes and entertainers can begin the necessary path to stewardship is to set up, through the unions, a formal trust fund that gives a percentage of their income to an organization dedicated to the coordination and execution of building a coalition of conscience. Granted, individual charities and organizations on the part of athletes and entertainers already exist; however, the key is having an organized and dedicated movement that brings financial and human resources together so social responsibility is not a momentary act of kindness, but rather a way of life.

KING MAKER: SHAPING CULTURE

A mind-shift must occur with respect to athletes and entertainers; this is one of the outstanding benefits in researching King's leadership with athletes and entertainers. By revisiting the depths of King's leadership with athletes and entertainers, researchers will discover that King shattered the notion that athletes and entertainers made their most valuable contributions to society by performing on athletic fields or stages. Before King, men and women in professional sports and entertainment did not see themselves as partners in the nation's struggle to address equality. King's leadership qualities during the Civil Rights Movement changed the nature of celebrity status. Placed in the proper context and examination, this reality can serve as a motivating factor for athletes and entertainers to see the promise and potential of their involvement in social causes.

This mind-shift for athletes and entertainers requires a new measurement for success, one that requires self-discipline and self-development. King lived and called for others to embrace a revolution of values in which power and prestige would be used to shape the nation's focus to care for all Americans. As part of his revolution of values, King called the nation into global acts of service and nobility. His call to greatness expanded the boundaries of race, region, socioeconomic status, and occupation. This clarion call to others began with King's self-convictions and moral compass. Athletes and entertainers, like those from a generation ago, must come to the conclusion that their contributions to society can be immeasurable because of their influence. Belafonte, Gregory, Baker, Baez, Robinson, and others made personal commitments to move with King toward the betterment of the nation.

KING MAKER: SERVING OTHERS

King's legacy shows us that greatness cannot be measured by monetary contracts or box office ticket sales. Reality programs that depict the size of an entertainer's home, rather than what he or she is willing to sacrifice for the greater good of others, do not reflect prestige or honor. King warned his followers of the dangers of being consumed with material gain. King called athletes and entertainers to accept and practice a new form of greatness—one that was measured by a person's contributions to humanity, not by the amount paid for the purchase of a new vehicle. King wrote:

> "Everybody can be great. . . Because everybody can serve. You don't have to have a college degree to serve. You don't have to make your subject and your verb agree to serve. You don't have to know about Plato and Aristotle to serve. You don't have to know Einstein's theory of relativity to serve. . . You only need a heart full of grace. A soul generated by love. And you can be that servant."[86]

Often, athletes and entertainers are known more for contract disputes than for serving "the least of these," [87] such as the nation's poor. Some athletes and entertainers have demonstrated acts of social compassion. Yet, a void remains for a collective and continued struggle, led by civil rights organizations or individuals, which calls athletes and entertainers to shared sacrifice and social responsibility. King marshaled a united front to confront the issues of his time. Activism by one group or individual did not advance the Civil Rights Movement. King called for a "world-wide fellowship that lifts neighborly concern beyond one's tribe, race, and class. . . Nothing less, as King urged forty years ago, than an all-embracing and unconditional love will advance humanity forward.[88] This was his dream and passion.

KING MAKER: AN ACTION PLAN

King identified and successfully implemented strategies that involved athletes and entertainers. In short, King had a plan, and he was intentional in his efforts to implement that plan. He maximized the human and financial resources of athletes and entertainers. He used media at his disposal, and built a network of athletes and entertainers who responded to his invitation to sustain the movement.

In order to match or surpass King's example of leadership with athletes and entertainers, contemporary leaders need to have a plan. King kept athletes and entertainers informed. King used his communication skills to speak to athletes and entertainers about the benefits of their resources given to the movement. This allowed for those who were initially skeptical to support King and to embrace his ideas, while it affirmed those who were willing to commit to do more.

King maximized the use of his time. He was decisive in points of strategy. He flew across the country to deliver speeches, hold rallies, and conduct press conferences in order to bring awareness to the nation on matters of racial injustice. By doing so, King built the trust necessary to sustain relationships with supporters of the movement. Athletes and entertainers saw his commitment and willingness to sacrifice, which served as fuel for others to consider how they could contribute more to the movement.

The name King became synonymous with a cause

greater than himself. He lived his life with a sense of urgency and refused to believe that the inevitability of time was the best agent to bring redemptive change. Athletes and entertainers can maximize their time by dedicating their collective skills and talents to address issues of poverty, war, and improving race relations. Again, the key is that athletes and entertainers make focused and collective efforts. King mastered the art of coalition building and saw that the power of a plan could unite people to place their collective efforts toward creating a better future for all.

KING MAKER: FOCUSED TECHNOLOGICAL RESOURCES

The resources at the disposal of contemporary leaders are far greater than those with which he had to work. Communication and technology can be tremendous assets to social movements. Social media outlets, including Facebook, e-mail, Twitter, Instagram, Flash-mob experiences, Skype, and cable television allow information to be processed and distributed in seconds, versus days or weeks as with King. Distances have been reduced from miles to minutes. Regional conflicts or tensions become national news by virtue of a reporter's wireless device, not through a Western Union Telegram. Therefore, instructions for peaceful protests can be distributed in the United States and around the globe.

Recent events in Egypt are one of the most prominent examples. Government authorities attempted to silence the voices of protesters through fear, intimidation, and cutting off phone and internet services. However, wireless networks,

Twitter accounts, and foreign cable news networks brought the revolution for values to the world, values which included freedom of speech and economic rights. Dissidents expressed their demands by way of cyberspace, including blogging and posting things on the World Wide Web, while nonviolence was the collective method of protest.

Despite the presence of abundant financial resources and visibility, a coalition of conscience of the scale and impact of the Civil Rights Movement is nonexistent. To be sure, athletes and entertainers are not the only groups at fault. Some of the nation's leading civil rights groups have struggled to gain their moral voices in this new era of social change. Members of the King family, who are among those charged with continuing the legacy of their father, have been in the news with financial infighting and lawsuits against each other, rather than coalition building with athletes and entertainers. The perception, and arguably the truth, is that King's legacy, with respect to his leadership with athletes and entertainers, has not been implemented further than when he left it on April 4, 1968.

King's leadership with athletes and entertainers lends insight to a way forward in creating a new coalition. King created a practice of seeding and nurturing a circle of leadership around him. His most valued commodity was human resources. King's relationship with Belafonte during the Civil Rights Movement is the best example of the value King placed on human resources and nurturing other leaders. The Birmingham Campaign, the March on Washington, the 1964 and 1965 Civil Rights Acts, and the anti-war protest of the Vietnam War were among King's signature moments in the movement.

Belafonte was actively involved in all of King's

major undertakings. As an actor and activist in his own right, Belafonte was engaged in matters concerning racial injustice before he met King. What the two accomplished together, however, was far greater than what they could have achieved alone. Belafonte was the key link to King's relationship with popular figures. Leaders who aspire to influence athletes and entertainers to advance social movements must see the importance of relationships. Additionally, athletes and entertainers, as well as organizations that have a desire to redeem the soul of America, can do more when they form mutual partnerships.

King's legacy and leadership with athletes and entertainers during the Civil Rights Movement demand more from humanity, especially those within the United States. However, this will require more than desire. The athletes and entertainers discussed in this research, on balance, are from America, arguably the most affluent nation in the world. What was true in King's view a generation ago remains true today: America lacks a social vision in which the priorities of average citizens and leaders are aligned. King's words bear relevance today:

> "America, the richest and most powerful nation in the world, can well lead the way in this revolution of values. There is nothing to prevent us from paying adequate wages to school teachers, social workers and other servants of the public to insure that we have the best available personnel in these positions who are charged with the responsibility of guiding our future generations."

King's leadership provides immeasurable insight into the realities of what can happen today when civil rights activists partner with two of the most influential groups in society: athletes and entertainers. He set the precedent for inviting athletes and entertainers to take up worthwhile causes, as he realized they were our nation's most influential figures.

Remember, U2's Bono had a dream of helping the world's poorest billion people, so he set up meeting with Jesse Helms. What dream do you have? What meeting do you need to set up? You can help forge the emergence of a new coalition of conscience where concerned citizens of goodwill use their influence to address the issues of today. There are King Makers all around you. Connect with one today or allow your King-Maker call to take flight. King's dream of equality regardless of ethnicity, race, and social status has been deferred. Don't let the dream go deferred any longer.

> " Life's most persistent and urgent question is,
> ' What are you doing for others?'
>
> – Dr. Martin Luther King Jr.

ABOUT THE AUTHOR
MARCUS "GOODIE" GOODLOE, Ph.D.

Marcus "Goodie" Goodloe was born in South Central Los Angeles, in the city of Compton, California. He attended Centennial High School and was offered full-athletic scholarships from multiple universities around the nation; he selected the University of New Mexico. Goodie was active in student and local government, serving as student regent and student body president in college, as well as a regional coordinator for a national presidential campaign. He served as Co-Coordinator for the National College Voter Registration Day, Co-Founder of the University of New Mexico Gospel Choir, and Co-Founder of the University's Black History Extravaganza.

Goodie was listed in colleges and universities "Who's Who in America," was collegiate Academic-All-American, and was a sports broadcaster for Q-13 News (a CBS affiliate). He was a nominee for Albuquerque's People's Choice Award, a recipient of the NAACP Gold Medal Award of Merit for outstanding leadership, and he is a graduate of the William and Mary African Leadership Institute. He graduated in 1994 with a Bachelor of Arts in Political Science, where he received the Clauve Outstanding Senior Award, presented annually to graduating seniors based on leadership, significant contributions to UNM and the surrounding community, as well as academic excellence. In 1997, Goodie earned a Master of Divinity from Golden Gate Baptist Theological Seminary in San Francisco, California. While enrolled at Golden Gate Seminary, he served as Target Group Recruiter and was a member on the President's Leadership Council; Goodie was the recipient of the Presidential Leadership Award for Excellence (the only award given at the seminary's graduation). Goodie concurrently served as Youth Pastor at the historic Allen Temple, a Church in Oakland, California, under the pastoral leadership of Dr. J. Alfred Smith, Senior (1996-1999), and later as Youth Pastor at Oak Cliff Bible Fellowship, under Dr. Tony Evans (1999-2005). Goodie earned a Ph.D. from Dallas Baptist University (2011; the first African-American to be awarded such), and was the graduation day's commencement speaker; Goodie's area of research was in leadership and social movement theory, with a focused concentration on the legacy and influence of Dr. Martin Luther King, Jr. with athletes and entertainers during the Civil Rights Movement, 1954-1968.

Goodie has been a regular lecturer for Youth Specialties, and a national speaker for the Student Song of Solomon, a biblical teaching series on attraction, dating, courtship, and marriage. In May 2006, he joined AWAKEN a team who specialize in the field of developing and unleashing personal and organizational creativity", founded by Mosaic's, Erwin McManus. Since 2008, Goodie has been the featured speaker for major professional and college sports teams and organizations including the Oakland Raiders (Oakland, California), Athletes Performance (Carson, California), Oklahoma Sooners Football Team, The University of New Mexico Men's Basketball Team, the "Character Dinner" with the nation's top athletes as part of the culmination of their training in preparations for the National Football League draft (a partnership with Mosaic and Athletes Performance), and the United States Military. He served as the Campus Pastor for Mosaic's South Bay Campus, and was part of the leadership team, which influenced over two-thousand adult volunteers on a weekly basis (2006-2012).

Since 2012, Goodie has served as a guest lecturer and adjunct professor at several institutions including Golden Gate Seminary (Brea, CA.), Dallas Baptist University (Dallas, TX.), Fuller Seminary (Pasadena, CA.), Loyola Marymount (Los Angeles, CA.), and Pepperdine University (Malibu, CA). He has consulted with business and educational leaders on matters of leadership, team synergy, character formation, and strategic planning for enhancement of customer service, and staff diversity. Chick-fil-A, State Farm, Dallas Baptist University, Fellowship of Christian Athletes, the New Mexico Annual Conference Clergy Retreat and Leadership Initiative for Transformation, as well as Cru are among the organizations Goodie has worked with. At present Goodie serves as Teaching Pastor at Parkcrest Church (Long Beach, CA), and is an active volunteer of Wave Church, Los Angeles. He is an advid reader, golfer, and life-long Oakland Raiders, Los Angeles Lakers, and New York Yankees fan (truly committed). Goodie and his wife of seventeen years, Lucy, live in the Los Angeles area and have two children, Hannah Marie (age 13) and Joshua C.H. (age 11).

ENDNOTES

INTRODUCTION

1. Jesse L. Jackson Sr. "The Rainbow Coalition." Speech delivered: Democratic National Convention, San Francisco, California, July 18, 1984. Text taken from pbs.org/wgbh/pages/frontline/jesse/speaker/jesse84/speech.html

CHAPTER 1

2. Bordas, Juana. Salsa, Soul, and Spirit: Leadership for a Multicultural Age. (San Francisco: Berrett-Koehler, 2007), 4-5, 15.

3. Deuteronomy 15:15

4. Acts 2:17

5. Branch, Taylor. Parting the Waters: America in the King Years, 1954-63. (New York: Simon & Schuster, 1988), 30-32.

6. Carson, Clayborne. Editor. The Autobiography of Martin Luther King Jr. (New York: Time Warner Books, 1998), 232.

CHAPTER 2

7. Branch, Taylor. Parting the Waters: America in the King Years, 1954-63. (New York: Simon & Schuster, 1988), 185.
8. Ibid., 185.

9. Belafonte, Harry. Personal interview with Taylor Branch, March 6-7,1985. Taylor Branch Paper Collection. University of North Carolina, Chapel Hill. Retrieved by the author December 5, 2009.

10. Ibid.

CHAPTER 3
11. Proverbs 22:6

12. Carson, Clayborne. Editor. The Autobiography of Martin Luther King Jr. (New York: Time Warner Books, 1998), 234.

13. Ibid., 356

14. Baez, Joan. Personal interview with Taylor Branch, January 13, 1987. Taylor Branch Paper Collection. University of North Carolina, Chapel Hill. Retrieved by the author December 5, 2009.

15. For a broader discussion of King and the SCLC quest and mission to "Redeem the Soul of America," see Faircloth, Adam. To Redeem the Soul of America: The SCLC and Martin Luther King Jr. (Athens: University of Georgia Press, 1987).

CHAPTER 4
16. Bush, George. Decision Points. (New York: Crown Publishing Group, 2010), 149.

17. Ibid., 325.

18. Baer, Susan. "U2's Bono in Washington," Washingtonian.com. March 1, 2006. http://www.washingtonian.com/articles/people/u2s-bono-in-washington/
Bush, Bush. Decision Points. (New York: Crown Publishing Group, 2010), 341,348, 350.

19. Owens, Jesse and Paul Neimark. Blackthink. (New York: Pocket Books, 1970), 103.

20. Schwartz, Larry. "Owens Pierced a Myth." Sports Century. https://espn. go.com/sportscentury/features/00016393.html170

21. Owens, Jesse and Paul Neimark. Blackthink. (New York: Pocket Books, 1970), 105.

22. King Jr., Martin Luther. Letter to Marlon Brando, July 22, 1966. King Library and Archives (KLA). Martin Luther King Jr. Center for Nonviolent Social Change. Retrieved by author December 4, 2009.

23. Ibid.
24. Rowe, William L. Western Union telegram to Martin Luther King Jr., sent through Louis and Rowe Enterprises on July 10, 1965, King Library and Archives. Retrieved by the author December 5, 2009.

25. King, Jr., Martin Luther. Letter to Sammy Davis Jr., dated, July 16, 1965, King Library and Archives. Retrieved by the author December 4, 2009.

26. Ibid.

27. Ibid

28. Allen, Steve. Letter to Martin Luther King Jr., February 11, 1966, King Library and Archives. Retrieved by the author September 16, 2009.

29. Baker, Josephine Baker. Letter to Martin Luther King Jr., October 14, 1963, King Library and Archives. Retrieved by the author December 4, 2009.

30. King, Jr., Martin Luther. Letter to Josephine Baker, November 5, 1963, King Library and Archives. Retrieved by the author December 4, 2009.

31. Branch, Taylor. Pillar of Fire: America in the King Years, 1963-

65. (New York: Simon & Schuster, 1998), 190.

CHAPTER 5

32. Washington, Jr., James M. Editor. A Testament of Hope: The Essential Writings and Speeches of Martin Luther King Jr. (San Francisco: HarperCollins, 2003), 85-90.

33. Branch, Taylor. Interview with Harry Belafonte, March 6-7, 1985. King Library and Archives. Retrieved December 5, 2009.

34. King Jr., Martin Luther. Letter to Burt Lancaster, April 27, 1965. King Library and Archives. Retrieved by author December 4, 2009.
King Jr., Martin Luther. Letter to Eartha Kitt, December 12, 1962. King Library and Archives. Retrieved by author December 4, 2009.

35. Robinson, Jackie. Letter to Martin Luther King, Jr., October 9, 1962. King Library and Archives. Retrieved by the author September 17, 2009.

CHAPTER 6

36. Luke 2:51-52

37. Branch, Taylor. Parting the Waters: America in the King Years, 1954-63. (New York: Simon & Schuster, 1988), 131.

38. Ibid., 138.

39. For broader discussion on the concept of "True North," see Covey, Stephen. The 7 Habits of Highly Effective People: Powerful Lessons in Personal Change. 25th Anniversary Edition. (New York: Simon & Schuster, 2013).

40. Branch, Taylor. At Canaan's Edge: America in the King Years, 1965-68. (New York: Simon & Schuster, 2005), 24.
Hall, Simon. Peace and Freedom: Civil Rights and Antiwar Movements. (Philadelphia: University of Pennsylvania, 2005), 26, 42.

41. Ibid.

42. Branch, Taylor. At Canaan's Edge: America in the King Years, 1965-68. (New York: Simon & Schuster, 2005), 591.
Carson, Clayborne. Editor. The Autobiography of Martin Luther King Jr. (New York: Time Warner Books, 1998), 33.
King Jr., Martin Luther. Where Do We Go from Here: Chaos or Community? (New York: Harper & Row, 1967), 35.

43. West, Cornell. The Cornell West Reader. (New York: Civita Books, 1999), 433.

44. Russell, Bill. "Comments." Sports Illustrated. June 6, 1967, 171-2. King Library and Archives. Retrieved by the author December 4, 2009.

45. Carson, Clayborne. Editor. The Autobiography of Martin Luther King Jr. (New York: Time Warner Books, 1998), 365-66.

46. Ibid., 220

CHAPTER 7

47. 1 Timothy 6:10

48. Carson, Clayborne. Editor. The Autobiography of Martin Luther King Jr. (New York: Time Warner Books, 1998), 174.
Garrow, David. Martin Luther King Jr., and the Southern Christian Leadership Conference. (New York: Harper Collins, 1986), 288.

49. Dyson, Michael Eric. Debating Race: with Michael Eric Dyson. (New York: Basic Civitas Books, 2007), 44.
Fairclough, Adam. Race and Democracy: The Civil Rights Struggle in Louisiana, 1915-1972. (Athens, Georgia: University of Georgia Press, 1999), 319.

50. Phillips, Donald. Martin Luther Jr., On Leadership: Inspiration and Wisdom for Challenging Times. (New York: Warner Books, 1999), 162.

51. Carson, Clayborne. Editor. The Autobiography of Martin Luther Jr. (New York: Time Warner Books, 1998), 206.
Washington Jr., James M. Editor. A Testament of Hope: The Essential Writings and Speeches of Martin Luther King Jr. (San Francisco: HarperCollins), 546.

52. King Jr., Martin Luther. Why We Can't Wait. (New York: Harper & Row, 1964), 57.
Branch, Taylor. Parting the Waters: America in the King Years, 1954-63. (New York: Simon & Schuster, 1988), 706.

53. King Jr., Martin Luther. Why We Can't Wait. (New York: Harper & Row, 1964), 68.

54. Ibid., 68.

55. Carson, Clayborne. Editor. The Autobiography of Martin Luther King Jr. (New York: Time Warner Books, 1998), 174.
King Jr., Martin Luther. Why We Can't Wait. (New York: Harper & Row, 1964), 58.
Branch, Taylor. Parting the Waters: The King Years, 1954-63. (New York: Simon & Schuster, 1988), 690.

56. Financial ledger. "Financial Report of City Rallies," of SCLC in 1963. King Library and Archives. Retrieved by the author

December 5, 2009.
57. Ibid.

58. Ibid.

59. King Jr., Martin Luther. Why We Can't Wait. (New York: Harper & Row, 1964), 68.

60. Financial ledger. "Financial Report of City Rallies," of SCLC in 1963. King Library and Archives. Retrieved by the author December 5, 2009.

61. Ibid.

62. Ibid.

CHAPTER 8

63. Washington Jr., James M. Editor. A Testament of Hope: The Essential Writings and Speeches of Martin Luther King Jr. (San Francisco: HarperCollins), 277.

64. King issued a statement in support of the rally: "Statement of Dr. Martin Luther King, Jr., President of SCLC, Atlanta Georgia," read by Arch McGucken in Francisco, California May 26, 1964. King Library and Archives. Retrieved by the author September 21, 2010.
Levy, Shawn. Paul Newman: A Life. (New York: Three Rivers Press, 2009), 185.

65. Ibid.

66. A handful of white players vocalized their support of the boycott; among them was Jack Kemp, quarterback of the Buffalo Bills. Kemp went on to become a U.S. Congressman and served as Secretary of Housing and Urban Development under President George H. W. Bush.

Wallace, William. "Race Issue Shifts All-Star Game from New Orleans to Houston; All-Star Game Goes to Houston." New York Times. July 12, 1965.

Mix, Ron. "Was This Their Freedom Ride?" Sports Illustrated. January 18, 1965, 24-25.

Bakers, William J. Sports in the Western World. (Totowa, NJ: Rowman & Littlefield, 1982), 290.

67. The change of venue was not the explicit decision of the players. Foss, who supported the players' position, made the decision as a compromise. For extensive discussion of the boycott: Smith, Maureen. "New Orleans, New Football League, and New Attitudes: The American League All-Star Game Boycott, January 1965." Sports and the Racial Divide: African-American and Latino Experience in an Era of Change. Ed. Lomax, and Kenneth Shropshire. (Jackson: University of Mississippi, 2008.), 2.

68. Garrow, David. FBI and Martin Luther King, Jr. from "Solo" to Memphis. (New York: Norton, 1981), 297.

James Chaney, Andrew Goodman, and Michael Swcherner were savagely beaten and shot multiple times. They were investigating church bombings in the South and had been part of the Freedom Summer movement, which focused on voter registration for African-Americans. On July 21, 1964, they shocked the nation and spoke about the risk all people of goodwill took to advance the civil rights agenda.

69. Sitton, Claude. "Mississippi Town Seizes 19 Negroes; Dick Gregory, Not Held, Leads Greenwood March," New York Times. Special 22. On-line. December 23, 2010. http://query. nytimes.com/mem/archive/pdf?res=FB0814FC3B5B12718DDD AD0894DC405B838AF1D3; Internet.
Branch, Taylor. Pillar of Fire: America in the King Years, 1963-65. (New York: Simon & Schuster, 1998), 151, 713.

70. McGraw, James. Interview with Dick Gregory: "What's Happening in Chicago," Renewal 8 (June 4, 1965). Series 1-12:16, King Library and Archives. Retrieved September 21, 2010.

71. Baker, Josephine. Telegram to Martin Luther King Jr., November 26, 1963. King Library and Archives. Retrieved by the author September 14, 2009.
Baker, Josephine. Telegram to Martin Luther King Jr., November 4, 1964. Retrieved September 14, 2009.
Baker, Josephine Baker. Telegram to Martin Luther King Jr., March 5, 1965. King Library and Archives. Retrieved September 16, 2009.

72. Micah 6:8, NIV

73. King, Coretta Scott. Editor. The Words of Martin Luther King, Jr. (New York: Newmarket Press), p.36

CHAPTER 9

74. King Jr., Martin Luther. Why We Can't Wait. (New York: Harper & Row, 1964), 94.
Washington Jr. James M. Editor. A Testament of Hope: The Essential Writings and Speeches of Martin Luther King, Jr. (San Francisco: HarperCollins), 296.

75. Branch, Taylor. Parting the Waters: America in the King Years, 1954-63. (New York: Simon & Schuster, 1988), 877.

76. Carson, Clayborne. Editor. The Autobiography of Martin Luther King Jr. (New York: Time Warner Books, 1998), 220.

77. Jones, Clarence B. Behind The Dream: The Speech That Transformed A Nation. (New York: Palgrave Macmillan, 2011), 105.
http://www.cnn.com/2015/08/12/us/north-carolina-mlk-jr-i-have-a-dream-recording/index.html

78. Carson, Clayborne. Editor. The Autobiography of Martin Luther King Jr. (New York: Time Warner Books, 1998), 122.
Garrow, David J. Bearing the Cross: Martin Luther King, Jr., and the Southern Christian Leadership Conference. (Norwalk, Ct: Easton, 1986), 273.

79. Branch, Taylor. Parting the Waters: America in the King Years. 1954-63. (New York: Simon & Schuster, 1988), 882.
Jones, Clarence B Behind The Dream: The Speech That Transformed A Nation. (New York: Palgrave MacMillan, 2001), 110, 113.

80. Ibid.175 176.

81. Ibid.

82. Zohar, Danah and Ian Marshall. Spiritual Capital: Wealth We Can Live By. (San Francisco: Berrett-Koehler Publishers, 2004), 87.

83. Paris, Peter. "Martin Luther King, Jr.'s Vision of America: An Ethical Assessment." Theology Today. 65, no. 1 (2008): 24.

CHAPTER 10

84. ESPN. "Content of Character." In Honor of Dr. Martin Luther King, Jr. 13 January 2011 [on-line]; accessed January 15, 2011. http://espn.go.com/espn/ feature/ index?page=mlkday
This was the culmination of a week of programming which played tributes to King.

85. Respers, Lisa. CNN France. http://www.cnn.com/2015/06/22/ entertainment/taylor-swift-apple-feat/

86. King, Coretta Scott. The Words of Martin Luther King Jr. (New York: New Market Press, 1987) 3.

87. King Jr., Martin Luther. Where Do We Go from Here: Chaos or Community? (New York: Harper and Row, 1967), 188.

88. Ibid., 190.

89. Ibid., 188.

FOR MORE INFORMATION, BOOKINGS, OR TO JOIN THE KINGMAKER MOVEMENT LOG ON TO:

KINGMAKERMOVEMENT.COM

CPSIA information can be obtained
at www.ICGtesting.com
Printed in the USA
FSOW03n1339191015
12243FS